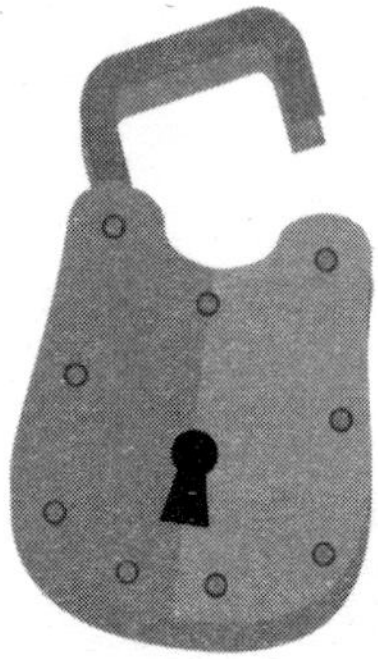

First published in Great Britain in 2024
by Red Shed, part of Farshore

HarperCollins*Publishers*
1 London Bridge Street, London SE1 9GF
www.farshore.co.uk

HarperCollins*Publishers*
Macken House, 39/40 Mayor Street Upper
Dublin 1, D01 C9W8

Red Shed is a registered trademark of
HarperCollins*Publishers* Ltd.

Puzzles on pages 18, 26, 32, 46, 50, 58, 70, 74, 78, 88, 92,
96, 112, 116 and 120 by Clarity Media Ltd

Maze on page 127 by Maze Generator

ISBN 978 0 00 872276 0

Printed and bound in the UK using 100% Renewable Electricity
at CPI Group (UK) Ltd.
001

A CIP catalogue record for this title is available from the British Library.

CASEY CLOSED

WHODUNNIT HIGH

RED SHED

CONTENTS

WELCOME TO WHODUNNIT HIGH – THE SCHOOL WHERE PERPLEXING PUZZLES AND CURIOUS CONUNDRUMS ARE THE NAME OF THE GAME.

So, you've sharpened your pencils, packed your rucksack and saved your new timetable . . . but little do you know that when you walk through the school gates for the first time, you'll be entering a world where mystery reigns supreme, and things are not quite as they seem . . . puzzles and mysteries keep cropping up, from the canteen and coat racks to the classrooms.

But help is at hand! Four students at the school love nothing more than a good puzzle to crack. They have taken you under their wing to show you around the school and get your help solving some of the baffling mysteries that are appearing.

Let's get to know them, and some of the other teachers and students . . .

???

SASHA

Hair colour: Red
Siblings: One older sister, one younger brother
Favourite subject: Biology
Wants to be: A vet
Ideal lunch: Chicken salad wrap
Super skill: Doing a brilliant impression of a T. rex

???

MAE

Hair colour: Brown
Siblings: Two younger sisters
Favourite subject: Geography
Wants to be: A volcano expert
Ideal lunch: Cheese and tomato sandwich
Super skill: Reciting the alphabet backwards

ANGELO

Hair colour: Brown
Siblings: None
Favourite subject: Art
Wants to be: An illustrator
Ideal lunch: Tomato soup
Super skill: Drawing bicycles

?

RAHIM

Hair colour: Black
Siblings: One younger brother
Favourite subject: History
Wants to be: An archaeologist
Ideal lunch: Cheesy baked potato
Super skill: Winning at rock, paper, scissors

?

HEAD TEACHER: MS SINGH

Likes: Crosswords, cycling
Dislikes: Whodunnit High's rusty bike shed

P.E. TEACHER: MS JACOBS

Likes: Early morning runs
Dislikes: Celery, heights

???

IT TEACHER: MR NELSON

Likes: Tidy desktop folders, cooking for his husband
Dislikes: Cold weather

CLASS TEACHER: MR CHAUDRY

Likes: Gardening, walking his dog
Dislikes: Neon colours

CLASS TEACHER: MRS PAGE

Likes: The seaside, sunny Saturdays
Dislikes: Hoovering, spiders

MUSIC TEACHER: MR GREEN

Likes: Ballroom dancing, cheering at his daughter's swimming competitions
Dislikes: Chocolate fingers, out-of-tune singing

LIBRARIAN: MS MUYUMBA

Likes: Fish finger sandwiches, pin badges
Dislikes: Untidy desks

???

RECEPTIONIST: MR BURR

Likes: New stationery, theatre shows
Dislikes: Scary films

THE LUNCHBOX MYSTERY – PART 1

DING DING DING DING!

The lunch bell rang out, and a throng of people wandered towards the lunch hall, along with the sound of rumbling stomachs. Mae picked up her lunchbox on the way.

Wait a second . . . it DEFINITELY felt lighter than it had that morning. Was there a lunch thief on the loose?!

Mae thought back to packing the lunchbox. There had definitely been:

- a banana
- a cheese and tomato sandwich
- a boiled egg
- a raspberry yoghurt
- ~~a flapjack~~
- a bottle of water.

She opened the lunchbox to take a look . . .

Look at the lunch list on the opposite page again – try to remember as much as you can in 30 seconds. Then, cover it up and look at the image below.

What's missing from Mae's lunch?

For the answer, see page 130

THE LUNCHBOX MYSTERY – PART 2

Mae had solved the mystery of what was missing from her lunch . . . but she was no closer to working out *who* had taken it. The lunchbox thief was still at large!

As she pondered who the culprit might be, a note fluttered to the floor . . .

Soon, she realised that the identity of the thief was hidden in the note.

Can you help Mae to work out who it was?

MY LUNCH WAS DISAPPOINTING
I JUST COULDN'T RESIST
AFTER I SAW YOURS.

BEFORE YOU GET TOO ANGRY
READ THIS NOTE CAREFULLY.
OFTEN LETTERS HOLD CLUES . . .
WHEN YOU KNOW MY
NAME, FIND ME SO I CAN SAY SORRY!

Hint:
TRY LOOKING AT THE
START OF EACH LINE.

It was time to confront them! Mae headed off to the playground, and the spot she knew the person usually sat.

For the answer, see page 130

THE MUSIC CLUB MYSTERY

It was time for jazz band practice! The room was filled with people busy polishing their instruments and joining in the gentle hubbub of musicians warming up.

As the music teacher Mr Green coached the trumpets, Angelo leant over to Rahim. "Here's a musical riddle for you . . ." he said.

What has lots of keys, but can't open any locked doors?

Rahim laughed – Angelo was full of tricky riddles, but this one he knew the answer to.

Can you work out the answer to the riddle?

Piano

Hint:

WHAT MIGHT ANGELO HAVE SEEN IN THE MUSIC ROOM TO INSPIRE THE RIDDLE?

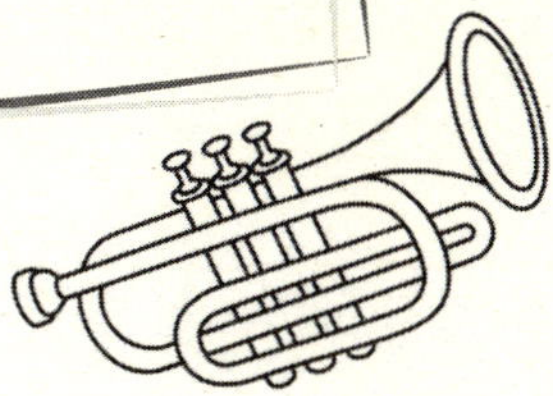

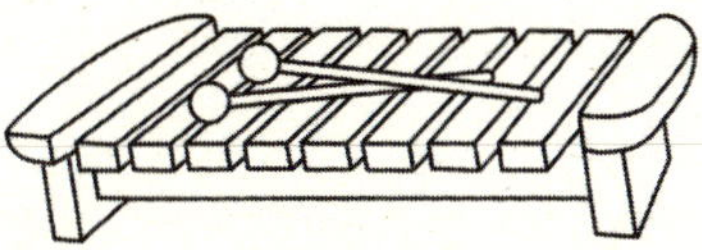

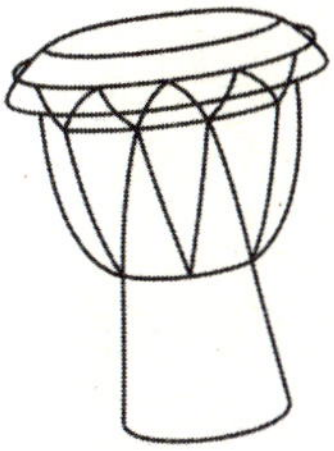

For the answer, see page 130

CROSSWORD COLLECTORS – 1

The headteacher of Whodunnit High, Ms Singh, was a big puzzle fan – no surprise there! She knew that Sasha, Rahim, Mae and Angelo loved doing puzzles, and one day, she presented them with a challenge . . .

"I've got five crosswords for you – I'll be giving them out one at a time. Once you've collected and finished them all, there will be a secret message to find. Just keep an eye on the shaded squares."

Solve the numbered clues, then put your answers into the boxes in the grid that start with the matching number. The 'across' clues go horizontally, the 'down' clues go vertically.

There are five crosswords in this book – collect the shaded letters from them all, then put them together in the order they appear to find a hidden word!

Across

1. Item used outdoors when it is raining (8)
6. Musical instrument you blow into (5)
7. Fast (5)
9. Smooth; level (4)
10. Evening meal (6)
12. Request strongly (6)
14. Nothing (4)
17. January, for example (5)
18. A state of quiet or calm (5)
19. Power (8)

Down

2. Small rodent (5)
3. To smell terrible (4)
4. State of matter between solid and gas (6)
5. Creature from outer space (5)
6. Liberty (7)
8. ______ machine, something you use to sing along with songs (7)
11. Item dropped by a ship to stay where it is (6)
13. Opposite of plus (5)
15. Very precise (5)
16. Not closed (4)

For the answer, see page 130

THE PRANK

As well as being brilliant puzzlers, Mae and Angelo were also experts at coming up with pranks to play on their friends. Sasha was one of their favourite targets.

Sasha had football practice at lunchtime on Thursdays – but she had realised that her football kit had mysteriously vanished.

She glanced at a mirror in the corner of the classroom and spotted Mae and Angelo reflected in it, giggling – everything clicked into place.

"You're the WORST. Give it back now, please."

"Hmm . . . that would be too easy," Mae replied. "We can give you this clue to help you look. You might need to look around for a tool to help you read it, though."

Mae handed over a crumpled note.

Can you help Sasha decipher the message and find out where her kit is hidden?

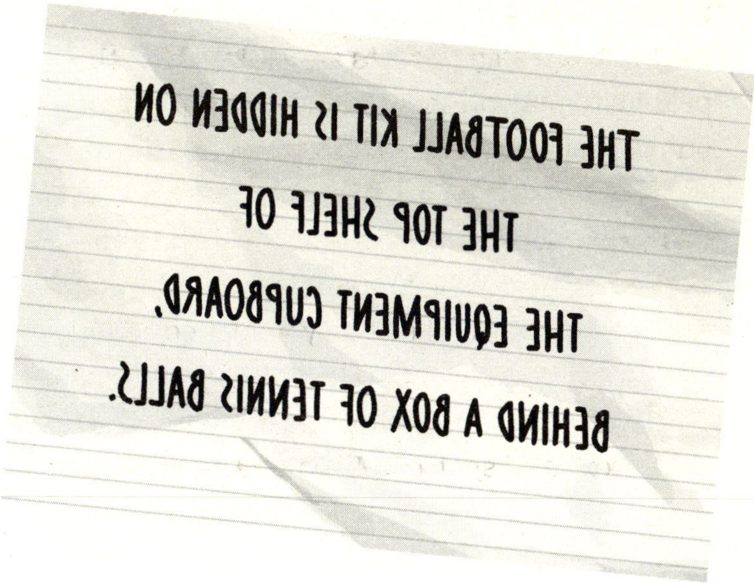

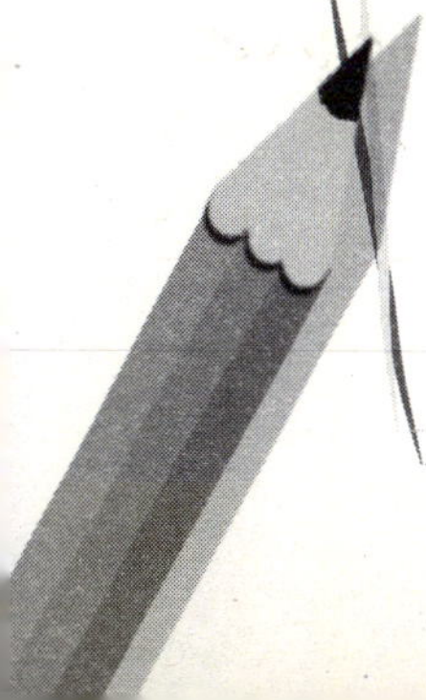

Hint:

WHAT OBJECT FROM THE CLASSROOM HAS SASHA ALREADY LOOKED AT ON THE OPPOSITE PAGE? HOW MIGHT IT HELP?

For the answer, see page 131

THE SECRET COPYARTIST

One morning, Angelo was heading to art class – his favourite subject. But when he got there, he noticed something mysterious . . .

One of the sketches on the wall had been copied, but with some differences added in. He could see ten differences between the two sketches.

Can you find all ten differences between the two pictures?

For the answer, see page 131

A MYSTERY LIST

During one afternoon's lessons, Rahim was sitting next to a girl named Hannah. He noticed that she was spending a lot of time during breaks jotting down notes in her exercise book.

Rahim got curious. "What's that you're making a list of?" he asked.

Hannah grinned. "Would you like to try my new word puzzle?"

"Yes please!" he replied.

Can you help Rahim work out what the words from list one have in common? Which word from list two could also fit into list one?

Hint:
WHAT DO YOU NOTICE ABOUT THE ORDER OF LETTERS IN EACH WORD? HANNAH'S NAME COULD ALSO FIT INTO THE FIRST LIST . . .

LIST ONE:

RACECAR
NOON
SOLOS
KAYAK
LEVEL

LIST TWO:

PENCIL
REDDER
TRAINS
SLIGHTLY
DATA

For the answer, see page 132

ART ADVENTURES

The four friends had created some brilliant drawings. Can you use the clues below to match each of the friends to the subject of their picture, the material they used and the colour of their artwork? Use the grid opposite to keep track of the information you have worked out.

CLUES:

- **Mae created her drawing in pencil.**
- **The picture of the red tiger was NOT drawn in pencil or felt tip.**
- **Angelo's picture was coloured in pink.**
- **The green drawing was done in oil pastel.**
- **Rahim drew an incredible self-portrait.**
- **Angelo drew a fruit bowl filled with tropical fruits.**
- **Sasha painted her picture in watercolour.**

		Colour				Material				Subject			
		Blue	Green	Pink	Red	Felt tip	Oil pastel	Pencil	Watercolour	Fruit Bowl	Self-portrait	Sunflower	Tiger
Child	Angelo												
	Mae												
	Rahim												
	Sasha												
Subject	Fruit bowl												
	Self-portrait												
	Sunflower												
	Tiger												
Material	Felt Tip												
	Oil pastel												
	Pencil												
	Watercolour												

FOR TIPS ON COMPLETING LOGIC PUZZLES, GO TO PAGE 156!

Child	Subject	Material	Colour
Angelo			
Mae			
Rahim			
Sasha			

For the answer, see page 132

AROUND THE WORLD RIDDLING

Mr Chaudry, one of Whodunnit High's class teachers, was teaching a special class about travel and the different ways people can explore the world.

"Where would you most like to travel, if you could go anywhere?" he asked.

Mae immediately started writing – geography was her favourite subject and she had a long list of places. Mr Chaudry chuckled, "When you finish that question, how about a riddle to think about?"

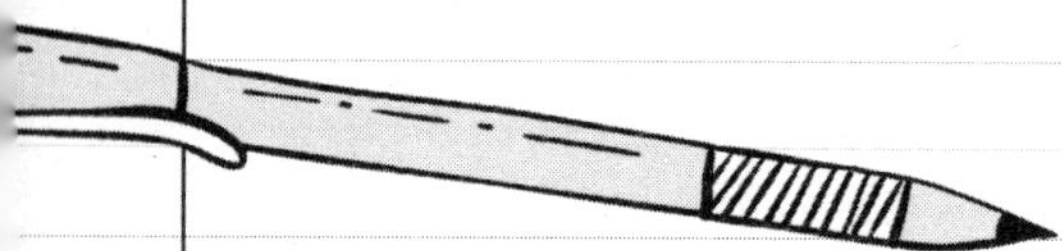

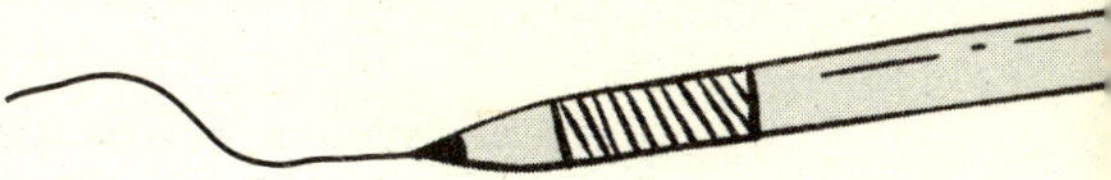

He wrote on the board:

What can travel thousands of kilometres to another country, while staying in its own corner?

Can you work out the answer?

Hint:
HOW MIGHT AN OBJECT BE SENT TO ANOTHER COUNTRY?

For the answer, see page 132

PAIR OF PENS

The four friends had been doing some homework together in the library after school but had lost track of time – it was about to close!

In Angelo's hurry to pack up, he swept his and Mae's pens into his pencil case. When they were safely out of the library, Angelo emptied the contents to sort them out.

"Don't worry," Mae said, "I had two pens and they were both identical. We just need to find the matching pair."

Can you help Angelo and Mae find the two pens opposite that are exactly the same?

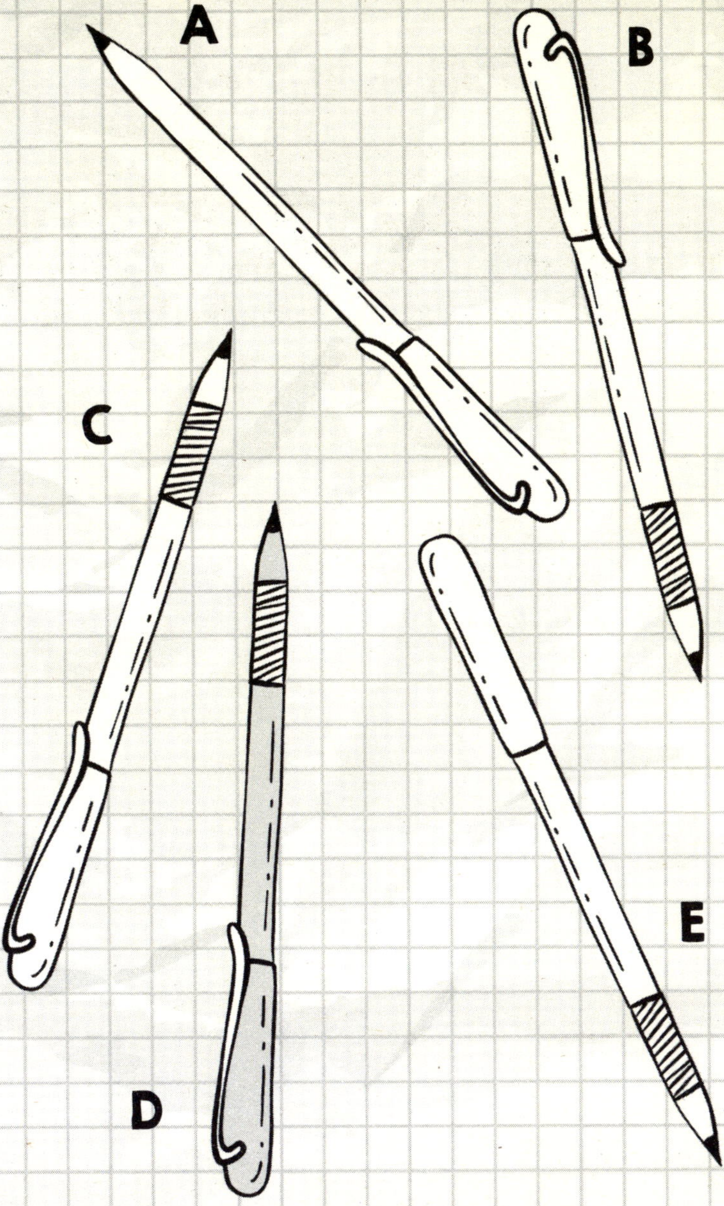

For the answer, see page 132

ANCIENT ADVENTURES

It was time for a Whodunnit High school trip – Sasha, Angelo, Rahim and Mae's class was spending the day at a museum, exploring the ancient Egyptian collection.

As they entered the museum and began gazing around at the vast stone columns and sparkling monuments in glass cases, Mrs Page handed round some sheets of paper.

"It wouldn't be a Whodunnit High trip without a puzzle to get you started . . . hidden in this wordsearch are 12 words, all to do with ancient Egypt. Can you find them all? All of the words are either hidden horizontally (across) or vertically (up and down)."

Can you complete the wordsearch?

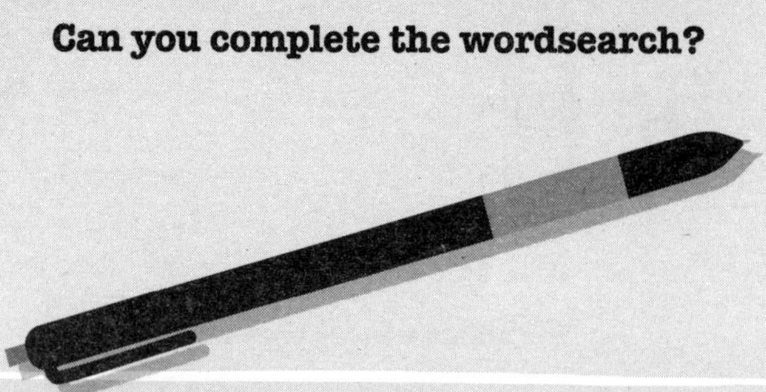

T	E	A	K	J	V	E	S	I	N	R	L
M	S	P	H	I	N	X	C	S	I	E	O
T	J	X	Z	P	S	I	A	F	L	C	B
P	H	A	R	A	O	H	R	O	E	H	E
M	D	P	B	P	H	H	A	M	Y	N	L
P	O	T	L	Y	P	X	B	Y	P	R	I
Y	H	I	E	R	O	G	L	Y	P	H	S
R	M	A	V	U	Y	C	Y	S	G	Y	K
A	U	D	E	S	E	R	T	I	V	E	H
M	M	L	C	R	O	C	O	D	I	L	E
I	M	Z	L	R	R	P	G	S	U	R	A
D	Y	E	P	J	A	C	K	A	L	P	E

CROCODILE
DESERT
HIEROGLYPH
JACKAL
MUMMY
NILE
OBELISK
PAPYRUS
PHARAOH
PYRAMID
SCARAB
SPHINX

For the answer, see page 133

MORSE CODE

It was time for a history lesson – but with a Whodunnit High twist. It was the history of codes and secret messages!

The four friends' class teacher Mrs Page began to explain.

"In the 1800s, a new code was invented to send messages over long distances – the alphabet was encoded by replacing each letter with a pattern of dots and dashes. It was called Morse code, after its inventor, Samuel Morse. This is what it looked like."

She handed out a sheet of paper:

A = .-	B = -...	C = -.-.	D = -..
E = .	F = ..-.	G = --.	H = ...
I = ..	J = .---	K = -.-	L = .-..
M = --	N = -.	O = ---	P = .--.
Q = --.-	R = .-.	S = ...	T = -
U = ..-	V = ...-	W = .--	X = -..-
	Y = -.--	Z = --..	

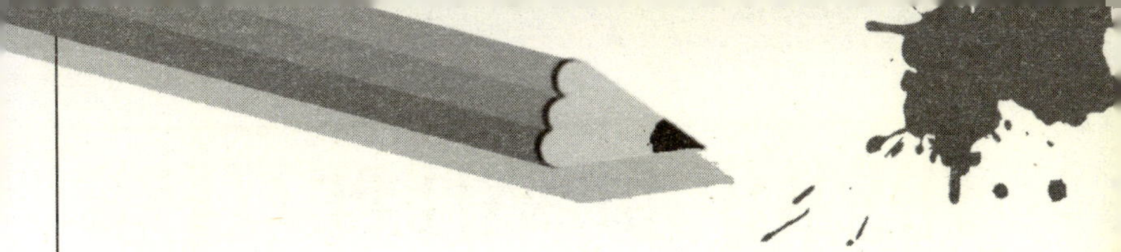

She also added, "Samuel Morse wasn't just an inventor – he also had another profession. I've coded it on the board using Morse code."

.-	.--.	.-	..	-.	-	.	.-.

Can you decode this message using the code opposite to find out what Samuel Morse's other profession was?

Try using Morse code to send secret messages to your friends. Or you could make up your own code using different arrangements of dots and dashes, or even different shapes.

For the answer, see page 133

THE WHODUNNIT PUZZLER

EDITION 1

Welcome to your favourite school newspaper.
All the news! All the updates! All the PUZZLES!

PET PANDEMONIUM!

Yesterday was Bring Your Pet to School Day at Whodunnit High – AND IT WAS CHAOS! Mia Brown's kitten snuck into the headteacher's office and was sick on her desk. Tom Bryan's chameleon, Flash, disappeared for the whole day. Flash was finally discovered in the library, sitting on a book about . . . chameleons! All pets are now safely back home. Did you and your pet take part? Send us your stories!

PET OF THE DAY

Mrs Whiskers belongs to Mr Burr, our school receptionist. She's almost 15 – pretty old for a cat. Mr Burr says: "Mrs Whiskers loves tuna and tummy rubs. She's always waiting for me on the fence when I get home – even when it's raining." Aw!

AND NOW FOR SOME ANIMAL-THEMED PUZZLES . . .

These three sets of animals have had their names scrambled into anagrams. Can you rearrange the letters to reveal the animals?

1. PETS

OGD

ACT

SEOHR

IABRBT

MESUO

2. WILD LAND ANIMALS

AEGIFFR

ABER

EGIRT

ILNO

AADNP

3. OCEAN ANIMALS

SRHKA

OOTPSUC

LWHEA

DOHLNPI

UTRETL

For the answer, see pages 133–134

JIGSAW CHALLENGE

Whodunnit High has a great collection of jigsaw puzzles. Sometimes, though, the right piece can be hard to find . . . Can you spot which two pieces complete the jigsaw puzzle opposite? The correct pieces have been rotated.

For the answer, see page 134

EMOJI CODE

Inventing codes and secret ways of hiding messages is a favourite activity for the four friends. One afternoon, Sasha came up with a new code for the rest of the group.

"I've replaced each letter of the alphabet with an emoji – here's the full set."

"Here are five words encoded using my emoji code. Can you work out what they are? One of the coded words is an odd one out – can you work out which one doesn't fit with the others?"

1. 

2. 

3. 

4. 

5. 

Can you help Rahim, Mae and Angelo decode the words and find the odd one out? Then, try making your own secret message!

For the answer, see page 134

IT ALL ADDS UP – PART 1

The four friends were on their way to their classroom when something strange caught their eye – it was a small box on a bench underneath some coat hooks. It seemed to be locked with a padlock . . . and there was a note on top of it:

UNLOCK ME – solve the sums to crack the four-digit padlock code!

First number:

20
– 2
÷ 3
+ 3

= ?

Second number:

4
x 4
+ 4
÷ 10

= ?

Third number:

9
+ 3
x 2
− 9
÷ 5
= ?

Fourth number:

14
÷ 2
+ 3
x 2
− 12
= ?

Can you work out the code and unlock the padlock?

Hint:
USE A SPARE PIECE OF PAPER TO HELP YOU WORK OUT THE SUMS IF YOU NEED TO.

For the answer, see page 135

IT ALL ADDS UP – PART 2

Mae, Sasha, Rahim and Angelo arranged the padlock with the digits and the lock sprang open. They had cracked the code!

Neatly folded inside the box was a piece of paper – Rahim unfolded it and read to the rest of the group:

CAN YOU WORK OUT WHAT ANIMAL IS HIDING IN THIS RIDDLE?

YOU CAN FIND MY FIRST LETTER IN **SIT** BUT NOT IN **TIN**.

MY SECOND LETTER IS IN **SHOE** BUT NOT IN **SOLE**.

MY THIRD LETTER IS IN **LIE** BUT NOT IN **OIL**.

MY FOURTH LETTER IS IN **DOSE** BUT NOT IN **SODA**.

MY FIFTH LETTER IS IN **PAT** BUT NOT IN **TASK**.

Can you figure our the hidden animal? Look carefully at the letters of each word in bold.

Hint:

WHAT LETTER IN THE WORD 'SIT' CANNOT BE FOUND IN THE WORD 'TIN'?

For the answer, see page 135

LIBRARY LOGIC

Mae, Angelo, Sasha and Rahim each took out a book from the school library. Can you use the clues below to work out who the main character is for each book, where the story is set and what type of book it is? Use the grid opposite to keep track of the information you have worked out.

CLUES:

- One book tells the story of a writer lost in a forest.
- Mae's book is about an inventor.
- Sasha's book is set on a boat.
- The comedy book is set on a mountain.
- Rahim's book is about an explorer.
- Mae is not reading an action or comedy book.
- The non fiction book is NOT set in a forest.
- Angelo is reading a fantasy book.
- The action story is about an artist.

		Type of book				Setting				Main character			
		Action	Comedy	Non fiction	Fantasy	Boat	City	Forest	Mountain	Artist	Explorer	Inventor	Writer
Child	Angelo												
	Mae												
	Rahim												
	Sasha												
Main character	Artist												
	Explorer												
	Inventor												
	Writer												
Setting	Boat												
	City												
	Forest												
	Mountain												

FOR TIPS ON COMPLETING LOGIC PUZZLES, GO TO PAGE 156!

Child	Character	Setting	Type of book
Angelo			
Mae			
Rahim			
Sasha			

For the answer, see page 136

HOME TIME

It was nearly the end of the school day at Whodunnit High – and today, Angelo was VERY ready for it. Time seemed to have slowed down to a snail's pace . . .

"Psst!"

A voice interrupted his thoughts. It was Sasha – he saw her hand was clenched under the table. Before he knew it, she had passed him a crumpled note.

"You look like you need a riddle to get you to the end of the day," she whispered.

He opened it as quietly as he could and read the contents:

What has hands but cannot clap, wave or give a thumbs-up?

What do you think the answer is?

Hint:
WHAT MIGHT YOU LOOK AT IN A CLASSROOM TO CHECK HOW LONG YOU'VE GOT LEFT IN A LESSON?

For the answer, see page 136

CROSSWORD COLLECTORS – 2

It was time for Ms Singh's second crossword! (Go back to page 18 for the first one.)

Can you complete the crossword? Solve the numbered clues, then put your answers into the boxes in the grid that start with the matching number. The 'across' clues go horizontally, the 'down' clues go vertically.

Don't forget to make a note of the letter in the shaded box! There are five crosswords in this book – work out the shaded letter in each one, then put them together in the order they appear to find a hidden word.

Across

1. Sweet treat made from cocoa (9)
6. Father or mother's brother (5)
7. Unit of volume found on a bottle of water (5)
9. Part of the nose (7)
12. Where apples are grown (7)
16. Brother or sister's daughter (5)
17. Picture (5)
18. Cuddly toy (5,4)

Down

2. A single time (4)
3. Pacific or Atlantic, for example (5)
4. Book of maps (5)
5. Whole (6)
6. Mythical creature with one horn (7)
8. Make bigger; anagram of EARN LEG (7)
10. Item used to paddle a boat (3)
11. Receive willingly (6)
13. In the lead; not behind (5)
14. Every 24 hours (5)
15. Rescue (4)

For the answer, see page 136

OPPOSITES

Mae and Sasha had been having fun coming up with some word games for the rest of the group – today, it was all about opposites.

“There are four pairs of opposites in this list – but one word does NOT have an opposite.”

Can you find the word in this list that does not have an opposite?

NOISY
DRY
SHORT
BEST
FAST
WET
QUIET
TALL
SLOW

"You aced that," said Mae – how about this list? One more thing – if you put the two odd words out together, they describe our group!"

**Can you find the second odd one out?
What do the two words without opposites spell when you put them together?**

DARK
UP
ASLEEP
LOW
AWAKE
HIGH
FRIENDS
LIGHT
DOWN

???

For the answer, see page 137

ODD JUMPER OUT

It was the first warm spring day of the year at Whodunnit High, and during lunch, lots of the students had taken off their school jumpers while sitting outside.

It was time to head to class, but Sasha's jumper had got mixed up with a pile of others. Luckily, hers had one small difference . . .

Can you help Sasha find her jumper by spotting the one jumper out of the five that is not identical?

A

B

C

D

E

For the answer, see page 138

HIDDEN HABITAT

The four friends had been learning about different animal habitats around the world with their class teacher, Mrs Page.

"If I was an animal, I'd want to live in a snowy Arctic habitat," Angelo exclaimed as the class finished. "Where would you live, Rahim?"

But before he could answer, a paper plane flew across the room and landed in front of Angelo. On it was a message: SOLVE ME.

Angelo and Rahim weren't sure where it had come from, but they never said no to a puzzle! They unfolded it and read the message inside . . .

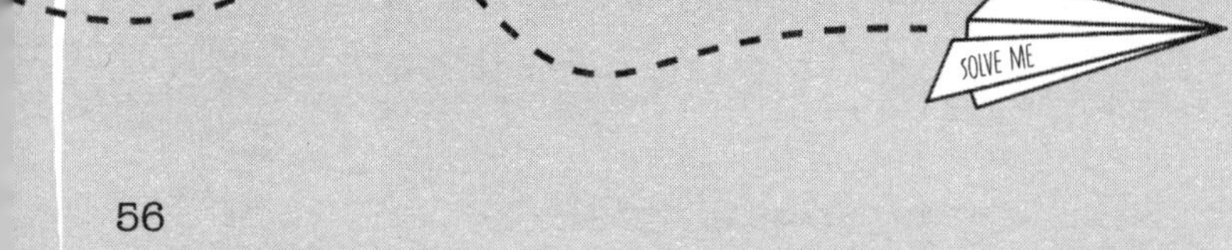

The words in this list each have a set of double letters (like the word LETTER) but the double letters have been removed. Can you use the clues to fill in the gaps? Make a note of each letter that has been doubled. What habitat do they spell?

1. L A _ _ E R

(Something you might use to climb up a wall)

2. S L _ _ P

(You usually do this at night)

3. S C I _ _ O R S

(A cutting tool)

4. K N _ _

(Part of the human body, in the middle of the leg)

5. M I _ _ O R

(You can use this to look at yourself)

6. K I _ _ E N

(A baby cat)

Hidden habitat: _ _ _ _ _ _

Can you help Angelo and Rahim find the hidden habitat?

For the answer, see page 138

EXPLORATION EXCITEMENT

Mae loves all things adventure! One day, she was flicking through a library book about deep-sea divers, when she came across a wordsearch all about explorers . . .

Can you help Mae finish the wordsearch? All of the words are either hidden horizontally (across), or vertically (up and down).

Bonus question:
Which tool from the wordsearch can you use to work out which direction is north?

G	A	D	T	E	L	E	S	C	O	P	E
C	O	U	R	A	G	E	X	D	S	Z	T
C	T	A	E	S	M	A	P	I	Z	F	T
O	V	O	A	U	Q	U	E	S	T	T	S
M	D	S	S	R	U	T	P	C	C	U	S
P	T	O	U	V	R	T	Y	O	P	I	A
A	A	G	R	I	C	U	J	V	Y	T	K
S	T	S	E	V	Q	G	R	E	F	S	Y
S	P	R	T	A	J	O	U	R	N	E	Y
G	F	C	O	L	E	U	Y	Y	E	E	A
W	M	M	O	U	N	T	A	I	N	L	R
V	O	Y	A	G	E	S	U	M	M	I	T

COMPASS
COURAGE
DISCOVERY
JOURNEY
MAP
MOUNTAIN
QUEST
SUMMIT
SURVIVAL
TELESCOPE
TREASURE
VOYAGE

For the answer, see page 139

A MYSTERY BOOK – PART 1

One day at Whodunnit High, Angelo had just sat down and started to unpack his schoolbag when he noticed a book that he didn't recognise on his classroom desk. It was a chunky book with a strap that wrapped around the front to lock the cover shut.

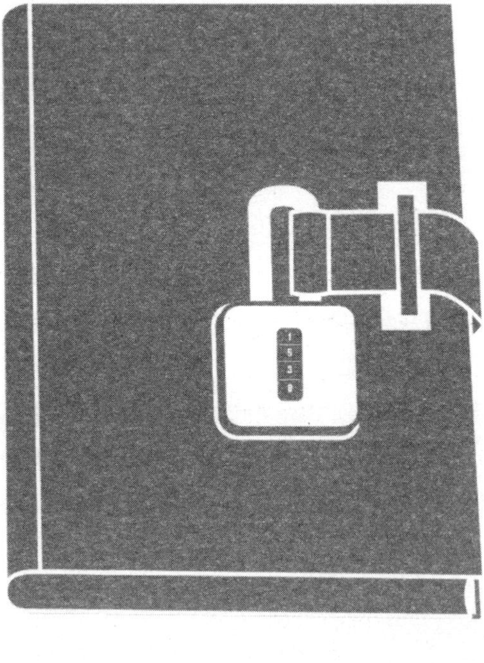

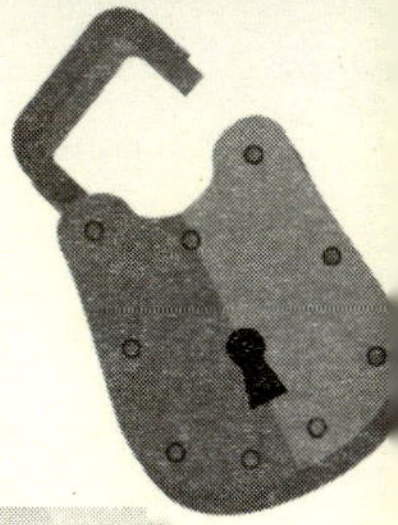

Stuck to the back, Angelo found a note:

REWARD FOR RETURN IF LOST!
FOR THE PADLOCK CODE, FILL IN THE GAPS
AND FIND THE CIRCLED NUMBERS:

1.	12	10	8	6	_	(_)
2.	_	(_)	12	15	18	21
3.	(_)	12	_	22	27	32
4.	2	4	(_)	16	_	64

Angelo had no idea who the book belonged to, but getting it open seemed like it might give a clue.

Can you fill in the gaps in each sequence? The numbers in the circles will be the padlock code.

For the answer, see page 139

A MYSTERY BOOK – PART 2

Angelo turned the wheels on the padlock so the circled numbers from the sequences lined up . . . click! It sprang open.

Inside, was written:
This book belongs to ____________ .

But there was no name! Just a grid . . .

I	R	Q	O	D	N
L	E	A	C	W	B
Z	D	E	H	P	S
T	E	J	I	●	E
N	A	E	M	K	R
★	F	E	E	G	L

. . . and a set of instructions:

Letter one:

- **GO TO THE STAR**
- **UP TWO SQUARES**
- **RIGHT THREE SQUARES**
- **DOWN ONE SQUARE**

Letter two:

- **GO TO THE CIRCLE**
- **LEFT THREE SQUARES**
- **RIGHT ONE SQUARE**
- **UP TWO SQUARES**

Letter three:

- **GO TO THE STAR**
- **UP ONE SQUARE**
- **RIGHT FIVE SQUARES**
- **UP ONE SQUARE**

Can you follow the instructions to reveal the name hidden in the grid, and uncover the owner of the book?

For the answer, see page 140

THE WHODUNNIT PUZZLER

EDITION 2

Welcome to your favourite school newspaper.
All the news! All the updates! All the PUZZLES!

COOKING UP A STORM

On Monday we had a visit from celebrity chef Kam Kuk. Kam showed us how to make courgette fritters, banana and coconut smoothie AND carrot ice cream. Yes, you read that right! He also grows fruit and vegetables and gave us his top tips for growing our own, even without a garden.

COMPETITION TIME!

Do YOU want to choose what's on the lunch menu? Pick up an entry form outside the school office to enter our special competition!

HAVE WE WHET YOUR APPETITE? TIME FOR SOME FOOD-THEMED PUZZLES!

These three sets of fruits have all had some letters removed. Can you work out what they are?

CITRUS FRUIT

1. L _ M _ N
2. O _ A _ GE
3. L _ M _
4. G _ A _ EFR _ IT

BERRIES

1. _ TR _ W _ E _ RY
2. R _ SP _ E _ R _
3. C _ ANB _ R _ Y
4. _ LUEB _ R _ _

TROPICAL FRUIT

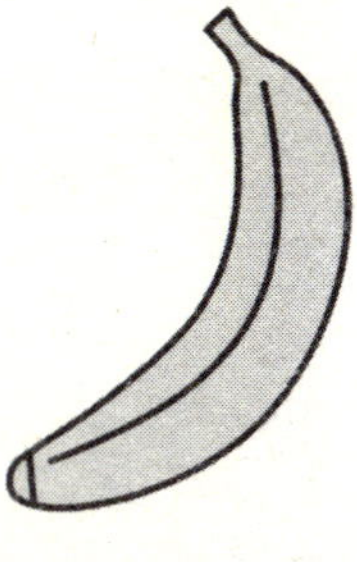

1. M _ NG _
2. W _ T _ RM _ L _ N
3. B _ N _ N _
4. P _ P _ YA

For the answer, see page 140

THE HIDDEN NOTE

On Wednesday lunchtimes, Sasha helps out in the school library, sorting out piles of books to be put back on the shelves.

During one of these sorting sessions, the librarian, Ms Muyumba, came over to her, holding a note.

"You work so hard, Sasha – I've got you a voucher for lunch in the canteen to say thank you for all your help. I also know how much you love puzzles . . . I've hidden the voucher inside a book and written you a few clues. Can you figure out which book it's hiding in?"

Sasha began to puzzle through the clues . . .

Can you figure out which book is hiding the voucher?

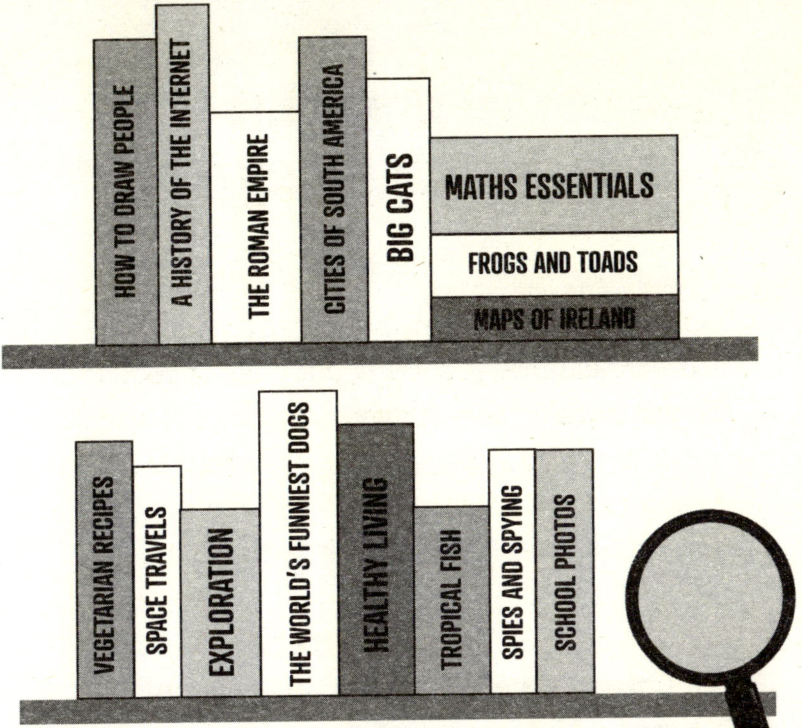

CLUES:

- **The book you need does NOT have an animal in the title.**
- **It is standing vertically on the shelf.**
- **There is a letter 'S' somewhere in the title.**
- **It is not at the end of a shelf.**
- **It has a two-word title.**
- **The book would not help you while cooking.**

For the answer, see page 140

QUIZ WIZARDS

Rahim had made a quiz for the others to solve – with a special twist . . .

He explained, "The answer to each question fits into the boxes opposite. Once you've found the answers, a secret word will be spelled out in the grey boxes, reading from top to bottom."

QUESTIONS:

1. Cobra, viper and anaconda are all types of what sort of animal?

2. How many sides does a hexagon have?

3. What colour paint would you get if you mixed red and blue together?

4. What is the name for a baby horse?

5. Which country is home to the Great Pyramid of Giza and the Great Sphinx?

Can you fill in the answers and work out what the hidden word is?

ANSWERS

1.

2.

3.

4.

5.

For the answer, see page 141

LUNCH LOGIC

Mae, Angelo, Rahim and Sasha have been looking forward to lunch all morning. Can you use the clues below to work out which sandwich, fruit and treat each of them has in their lunchbox? Use the grid opposite to keep track of the information you have worked out.

CLUES:

- Mae has a jam sandwich and an apple.
- Angelo's sandwich does not have ham.
- One friend has a peach and some chocolate in their lunchbox.
- Rahim's treat is either popcorn or a flapjack.
- One friend has a cheese sandwich and a cupcake in their lunchbox.
- The lunchbox with the apple in does not contain popcorn.
- One friend has a cucumber sandwich and an orange in their lunchbox.
- Mae's treat is a flapjack.
- Angelo has a kiwi in his lunchbox.

		Treat				Fruit				Sandwich			
		Chocolate	Cupcake	Flapjack	Popcorn	Apple	Kiwi	Orange	Peach	Cheese	Cucumber	Ham	Jam
Child	Angelo												
	Mae												
	Rahim												
	Sasha												
Sandwich	Cheese												
	Cucumber												
	Ham												
	Jam												
Fruit	Apple												
	Kiwi												
	Orange												
	Peach												

FOR TIPS ON COMPLETING LOGIC PUZZLES, GO TO PAGE 156!

Child	**Sandwich**	**Fruit**	**Treat**
Angelo			
Mae			
Rahim			
Sasha			

For the answer, see page 141

DOUBLE TROUBLE

Sasha has an older sister, who loves reading and learning new words. One day, Sasha came into school with a new challenge her sister had set for her.

"It's all about words that mean two different things," she said to the others. "Each of the two clues in each puzzle can be answered using the same word. Can you help me work them all out?"

Rahim, Mae and Angelo got to work – surely they could work them all out before the end of morning break . . .

Can you help them?

???

PUZZLE ONE

- A small animal with a long tail, sometimes kept as a pet.
- An object used to move a cursor on a computer screen.

Answer: _ _ _ _ _

PUZZLE TWO

- A nocturnal flying animal with leathery wings.
- Something used to hit a ball in sports such as cricket or baseball.

Answer: _ _ _

PUZZLE THREE

- A noise a dog might make.
- The outer layer of a tree trunk.

Answer: _ _ _ _

PUZZLE FOUR

- The small black circular part in the middle of your eye.
- A student at a school.

Answer: _ _ _ _ _

For the answer, see page 141

DEADLY DINOSAURS

Sasha loves any and all facts about the animal kingdom – that included dinosaurs! She was thrilled when the class went on a trip to visit a local museum to look at some dinosaur fossils.

As they were going round looking at the fossilised teeth and bones, the class were given a wordsearch.

Can you find all of the dinosaur-related words listed in the grid? All of the words are either hidden horizontally (across) or vertically (up and down).

Bonus question:
Which dinosaur from the wordsearch opposite had three horns on its face, that could be used to defend itself?

D	T	R	I	C	E	R	A	T	O	P	S
D	R	E	J	U	R	A	S	S	I	C	T
I	Z	P	R	E	D	A	T	O	R	S	E
P	T	E	R	O	D	A	C	T	Y	L	G
L	R	S	L	Q	C	N	D	F	T	R	O
O	I	G	U	A	N	O	D	O	N	A	S
D	A	N	P	U	L	N	S	S	L	P	A
O	S	C	L	A	W	S	V	S	Q	T	U
C	S	T	A	T	O	V	N	I	E	O	R
U	I	U	R	I	C	Z	R	L	W	R	U
S	C	L	E	P	P	U	N	R	F	T	S
O	X	E	X	T	I	N	C	T	Y	Z	Q

CLAWS
DIPLODOCUS
EXTINCT
FOSSIL
IGUANODON
JURASSIC
PREDATORS
PTERODACTYL
RAPTOR
STEGOSAURUS
TRIASSIC
TRICERATOPS

For the answer, see page 142

THE WHODUNNIT PUZZLER

EDITION 3

Welcome to your favourite school newspaper.
All the news! All the updates! All the PUZZLES!

HOLIDAY HOWLERS

It's almost time for the holiday! What are your best – and worst – holiday adventures? We asked class 6B to tell us theirs.

Mason Smith: "We went to the beach and I built a huge, AMAZING sandcastle with my brothers. Mum came over to look at it, but she tripped and fell on top of it. It was HILARIOUS!"

Finley Small: "We queued for an hour to go on the Questor ride at the theme park. When we finally got on, my little brother felt sick and we had to get straight off again. I was so disappointed!"

IF THIS HOLIDAY EDITION IS MAKING YOU WANT TO TRAVEL THE WORLD, YOU'LL LOVE TODAY'S PUZZLES . . .

The words in the three lists below have been split into two- or three-letter fragments, which have been rearranged. Can you put them back in the correct order to reveal the words?

SUMMER CLOTHES

1. OR SH TS
2. NH AT SU
3. ALS ND SA
4. ST VE
5. SU IM IT SW
6. NGL SU SES AS

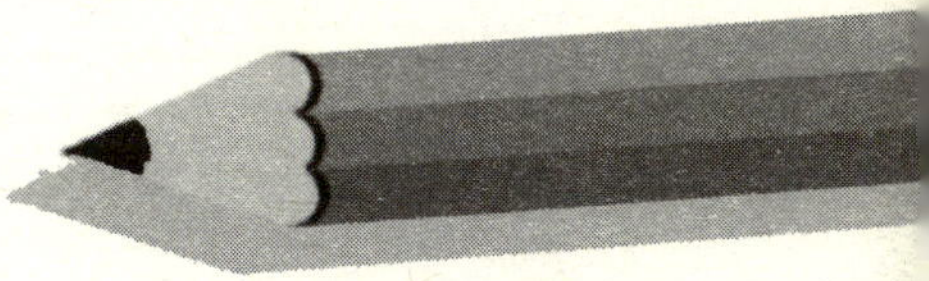

COUNTRIES

1. GE NI RIA
2. EN SW ED
3. NA DA CA
4. RA ST LIA AU
5. KIS PA TAN
6. ND LA PO

WEATHER

1. IN RA
2. OW SN
3. SU INE NSH
4. ND WI
5. DY OU CL
6. ARD BL IZZ

For the answer, see pages 142–143

CROSSWORD COLLECTORS – 3

Ms Singh has sent her third crossword! (See pages 18 and 50 for the first two.)

Can you help complete it? Solve the numbered clues, then put your answers into the boxes in the grid that start with the matching number. The 'across' clues go horizontally, the 'down' clues go vertically.

Remember to make a note of the letter in the shaded box! There are five crosswords in this book – find all the shaded letters, then put them together in the order they appear to find a hidden word.

Across

1. Source of irritation (8)
6. Great Barrier ___ : famous Australian sight (4)
7. One of the four seasons (6)
9. Where rabbits are kept (5)
11. Incorrect (5)
12. Vegetable that can make you cry (5)
13. Own up to (5)
16. Four times twenty (6)
18. The largest continent (4)
19. Part of a paragraph (8)

Down

1. Home of Santa Claus (5,4)
2. Incompetent; an anagram of IN PET (5)
3. Close by (4)
4. Went inside (7)
5. Meat from a pig (3)
8. Bad dream (9)
10. What people wear (7)
14. Someone who works with stone (5)
15. Religious song (4)
17. Frozen water (3)

For the answer, see page 143

TANGLED UP

Angelo, Sasha, Rahim and Mae were taking part in a craft session one morning – they each had a ball of wool that they were using to create colourful pom poms.

But, all had not gone to plan . . . Angelo had accidentally knocked over a box on the table, and their four balls of wool had flown onto the floor, and got very tangled.

Can you follow the strands of wool to work out which ball belongs to which person?

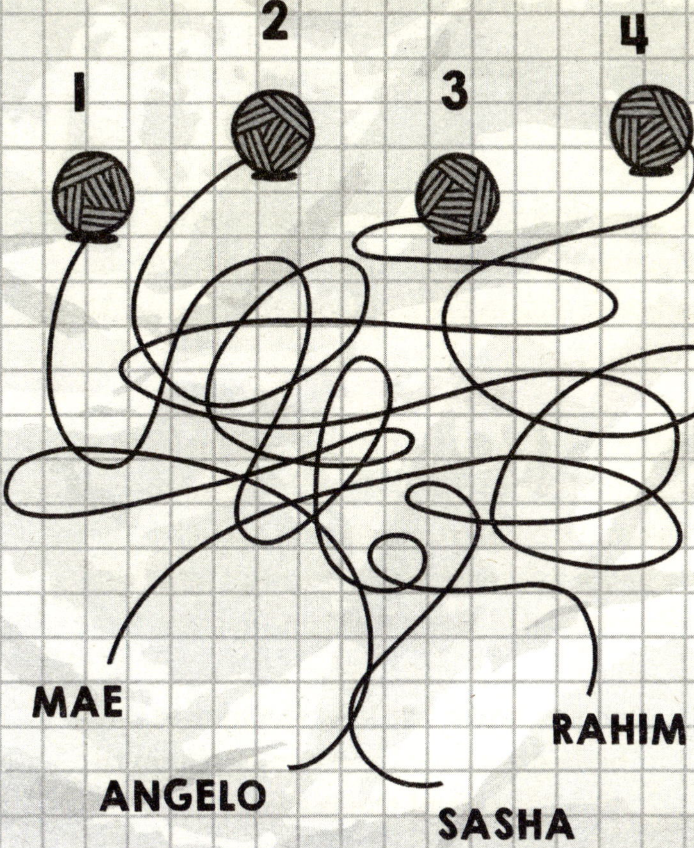

For the answer, see page 143

MINIBEAST MYSTERY

Rahim had spent his lunchtime reading all about amazing insects from around the world – he had been sharing lots of facts with Sasha, Mae and Angelo.

"Some insects can camouflage themselves to look identical to the bark of the trees they sit on. I've done a bit of camouflaging myself . . . here is a list of five insects that have all had their names encoded using the same system."

Can you work out how the names have been disguised, and decode them to reveal the insects?

PSAW

REPPOHSSARG

EEB

YLFRETTUB

OTIUQSOM

Hint:
TRY READING THE WORDS FROM
A NEW DIRECTION . . .

For the answer, see page 144

THE FINGERPRINTS

"Right, class – today, we're going to be looking at our own fingerprints."

The four friends grinned as their teacher Mrs Page announced the day's activity. She gave each table a piece of paper, and soon everyone was busily dipping their fingers into black paint, and then pressing them onto the paper.

Mae, Rahim, Angelo and Sasha's prints looked like this:

When everyone had finished, the large sheet was a mass of fingerprints. Angelo frowned . . .

"Hold on a second," he said. "There's one person whose prints aren't here at all."

Can you work out which of the friends has NOT added their fingerprint to the paper? Watch out – there may be some fingerprints there that do not belong to the four friends!

For the answer, see page 144

SHOE CONFUSION

It was time for P.E. with Ms Jacobs at Whodunnit High – but disaster had struck! Rahim, Angelo, Mae and Sasha all had very similar trainers, but they had all got mixed up in the changing rooms.

"We can solve this," cried Mae, "we're great at a puzzle! Each pair of shoes has at least one small difference – we've just got to match up the pairs."

Can you match up the trainers into their correct pairs? Each pair should have one left shoe and one right shoe.

For the answer, see page 144

CROSSWORD COLLECTORS – 4

It was time for Ms Singh's fourth crossword! (See pages 18, 50 and 78 for the first three.)

Can you complete it? Solve the numbered clues, then put your answers into the boxes in the grid that start with the matching number. The 'across' clues go horizontally, the 'down' clues go vertically.

Note down the letter in the shaded box! There are five crosswords in this book – find all the shaded letters across all of the crosswords, then put them together in the order they appear to find a hidden word.

Across

1. Fairy-tale princess (10)
5. Songs; what bands create (5)
7. Sharp point (5)
9. Person in charge (6)
10. Curve (4)
12. Reflection of a sound (4)
13. Opposite of top (6)
16. The name of a book (5)
17. Item you wear when cooking (5)
18. Book of words and meanings (10)

Down

1. Animal with a hump (5)
2. Go beyond (6)
3. Compass direction (4)
4. English city east of Birmingham; anagram of SECRET LIE (9)
6. Type of pasta (9)
8. Finish (3)
11. Root vegetable used to make chips (6)
12. Consume food (3)
14. Something you might keep in a bank account (5)
15. Where a bird lays eggs (4)

For the answer, see page 145

THE WHODUNNIT PUZZLER

EDITION 4

Welcome to your favourite school newspaper.
All the news! All the updates! All the PUZZLES!

DOG-NAV!

How's your memory? Noah Ferreira (Class 6M) knows someone with an INCREDIBLE memory: his dog, Beans! Last weekend, Noah and his family went away for the day and left Beans with his grandma. But Beans missed Noah so much that he ran out of the front door and all the way back to Noah's house . . . on the other side of town! Wow! Beans was waiting in the garden when Noah got home.

Noah's grandma said: "I looked all over the neighbourhood but couldn't find him. How did he remember the way? It's amazing!"

LUCKILY YOU DON'T NEED TO GO FAR TO EXERCISE YOUR MEMORY. TRY THESE PUZZLES INSTEAD . . .

Pick one of these lists of six words and take a good look at it for 30 seconds, trying to memorise as much of it as you can. Then, cover up the list, and see how many you can remember. Try testing a friend or family member too!

1. VEHICLES

- TRACTOR
- MOTORCYCLE
- TRAIN
- TRUCK
- HELICOPTER
- BUS

2. EMOTIONS

- HAPPY
- SAD
- EXCITED
- EMBARRASSED
- ANGRY
- LOVING

3. SPACE

- ROCKET
- ASTEROID
- PLANET
- COMET
- BLACK HOLE
- MOON

4. BIRDS OF PREY

- EAGLE
- OSPREY
- FALCON
- BUZZARD
- OWL
- HAWK

SPACE SOLVERS – PART 1

It was time for another Whodunnit High school trip – this time, they were heading out to an exhibition all about space and space travel.

While they were looking at the amazing rockets and fragments of space rock in the exhibition, the class were also busily working on some space-themed puzzles. It wouldn't be a Whodunnit High trip without them!

Can you help complete this space wordsearch? All of the words are either hidden horizontally (across) or vertically (up and down).

A	S	T	R	O	N	A	U	T	H	A	A
Y	M	S	S	T	A	R	F	R	T	R	N
T	O	U	O	A	S	T	E	R	O	I	D
S	O	P	U	B	M	P	T	R	H	F	F
P	N	E	P	L	E	Q	M	A	X	Z	I
T	O	R	S	A	T	E	L	L	I	T	E
D	G	N	X	C	E	O	E	I	B	R	O
I	A	O	U	K	O	N	O	R	B	I	T
U	L	V	T	H	R	S	M	I	U	L	V
I	A	A	P	O	I	Z	C	O	M	E	T
T	X	P	T	L	T	F	U	E	L	A	T
E	Y	E	V	E	E	P	L	A	N	E	T

ASTEROID
ASTRONAUT
BLACK HOLE
COMET
GALAXY
METEORITE
MOON
ORBIT
PLANET
SATELLITE
STAR
SUPERNOVA

For the answer, see page 145

SPACE SOLVERS – PART 2

The second puzzle the group had to complete while they looked around the exhibition was a space quiz. But not content with simply answering the questions, Mae had hidden a secret message in hers . . .

"I've circled a letter in each answer – can you answer the questions, and read the circled letters in order to reveal the hidden word?"

1. What is a person who travels up to space often called?

AN A _ _ _ _ _ (_) _ _

2. Jupiter, Earth and Mercury are all types of what?

P (_) _ _ _ _

3. What's the name for a small, rocky object that orbits the Sun in our Solar System?

AN A _ _ _ _ _ (_) _

4. What tool do astronomers use to look at far-away objects in space?

A T _ _ (_) _ _ _ _ _

5. Where did Neil Armstrong walk in 1967, becoming the first person to do so?

THE M _ _ (_)

For the answer, see page 146

AWAY ON HOLIDAY

Mae, Angelo, Rahim and Sasha were talking about their summer holidays. Work out which country each of them visited, what type of holiday they had, and what they brought back as a souvenir.

CLUES:

- One child had a beach holiday in Wales.
- Mae spent her holiday at a hotel resort in Scotland. She bought a pencil as a souvenir.
- Angelo either brought back a bracelet or a notebook as souvenir.
- Sasha spent her holiday in France.
- One child brought back a bracelet from Spain.
- The key ring was not bought at the beach.
- Angelo spent his holidays hiking.

		Souvenir				Type of holiday				Country			
		Bracelet	Key ring	Notebook	Pencil	Beach	Camping	Hiking	Hotel resort	France	Scotland	Spain	Wales
Child	Angelo												
	Mae												
	Rahim												
	Sasha												
Country	France												
	Scotland												
	Spain												
	Wales												
Type of holiday	Beach												
	Camping												
	Hiking												
	Hotel resort												

FOR TIPS ON COMPLETING LOGIC PUZZLES, GO TO PAGE 156!

Child	Country	Type of holiday	Souvenir
Angelo			
Mae			
Rahim			
Sasha			

For the answer, see page 146

THE LOST PENCIL CASE – PART 1

Angelo and Rahim had been walking along the corridor when they came across a pencil case lying on the floor. It seemed to be lost property – but whose could it be? When they had a look inside, there was no name label. All they could find was a note:

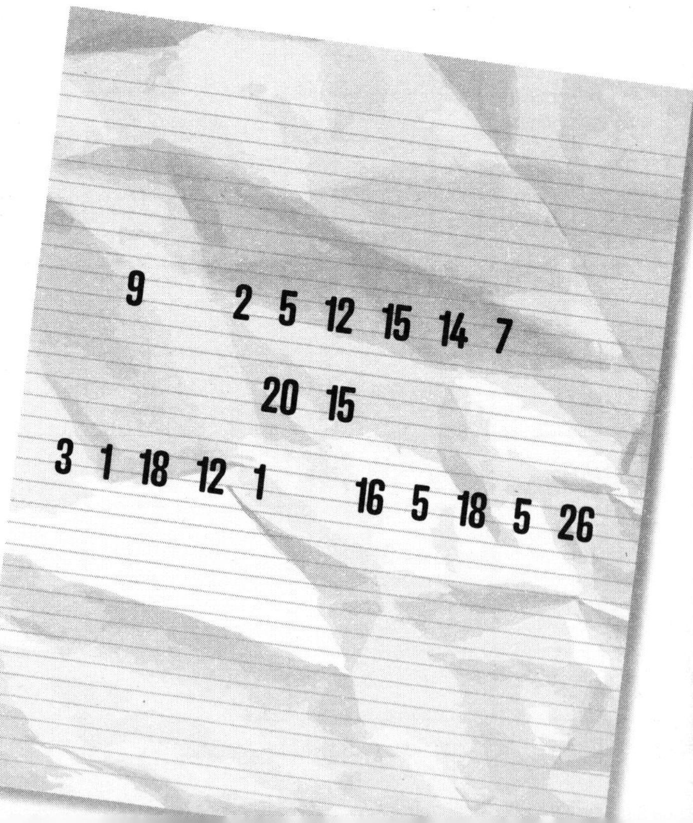

It must be a code! Rahim remembered hearing about a code where numbers were swapped for letters – could there be a message hidden behind the numbers? He quickly flicked through his notebook until he found the chart he had made.

Can you help decipher the message?
Use Rahim's code chart below to help you.

A	B	C	D	E	F	G	H	I	J	K	L	M
1	2	3	4	5	6	7	8	9	10	11	12	13

N	O	P	Q	R	S	T	U	V	W	X	Y	Z
14	15	16	17	18	19	20	21	22	23	24	25	26

For the answer, see page 146

THE LOST PENCIL CASE – PART 2

Angelo and Rahim found the pencil case's owner with your expert help – they were relieved to have it returned, and impressed with your code-breaking!

Angelo had been inspired by this new kind of code – he disappeared over lunchtime, and when he came back, he had a secret message of his own for Rahim . . .

Can you decode Angelo's message?

Hint:
ONCE YOU'VE WORKED OUT WHICH LETTER ONE NUMBER REPRESENTS, TRY FINDING ALL OF THE OTHER TIMES THAT NUMBER COMES UP IN THE MESSAGE.

23 8 1 20 7 1 13 5 4 15

3 18 15 3 15 4 9 12 5 19

12 9 11 5

16 12 1 25 9 14 7?

19 14 1 16!

A	B	C	D	E	F	G	H	I	J	K	L	M
1	2	3	4	5	6	7	8	9	10	11	12	13

N	O	P	Q	R	S	T	U	V	W	X	Y	Z
14	15	16	17	18	19	20	21	22	23	24	25	26

Try making your own secret message!

For the answer, see page 147

SPORTS CHALLENGE

Angelo and Mae were chatting after football practice when the teacher, Ms Jacobs, called them back.

"You two are good with a challenge – I need to count all the sports balls to make sure none are missing."

Can you count how many footballs, tennis balls and basketballs there are in the cupboard?

Bonus question:
What is the only type of ball with an even number in the cupboard?

For the answer, see page 147

SECRET NOTE

It was Rahim's birthday coming up and Mae was planning a present for him – talking to the others to make plans, though, was tricky when they were all in the same class . . . but at Whodunnit High, there were always secret messages to be sent!

She passed a note across to Angelo. "What do you think?" she whispered.

Can you work out the two gifts hidden in the note opposite? Use the clues below to help you.

PRESENT IDEA ONE: SQUARES.

PRESENT IDEA TWO: CIRCLES.

THIS IS A HIDDEN
MESSAGE - READ TO
FIND ALL THE TRUTH
YOU NEED.

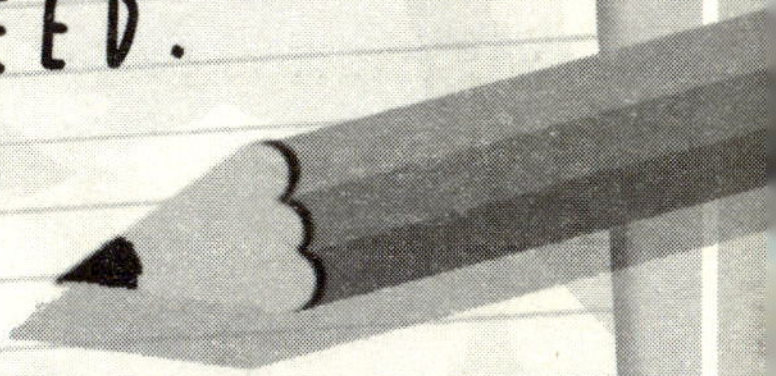

Hint:

CAN YOU SPELL OUT ANY WORDS BY
JUST READING THE LETTERS IN SQUARES?
WHAT ABOUT CIRCLES?

For the answer, see page 147

THE WHODUNNIT PUZZLER

EDITION 5

Welcome to your favourite school newspaper.
All the news! All the updates! All the PUZZLES!

QUIT MONKEYING AROUND!

Are you a budding zookeeper? Zoe Khan is! Zoe (Class 5C) was at Grange Park Zoo on Saturday afternoon when she spotted a small tufted capuchin climbing out of a hole in the netting of its enclosure. She immediately ran to find the zookeeper, who rescued the monkey.

The head zookeeper thanked Zoe for her quick thinking, saying: "Who knows what monkey business that little one might have got up to if Zoe hadn't spotted her!"

What's your favourite animal? Write and tell us!

TODAY'S PUZZLES ARE ALL ABOUT ANIMALS YOU MIGHT FIND IN A ZOO . . .

These facts are each missing a number – use the clues below each fact to discover the missing numbers and complete the facts.

1. AN OCTOPUS HAS ______ HEARTS.

(Number of hearts in this edition.)

2. A GREAT WHITE SHARK HAS AROUND ______ TEETH.

(Number of grey circles in this edition, multiplied by 100.)

3. A KOALA CAN SLEEP FOR UP TO ____ HOURS IN A SINGLE DAY.

(Number of question marks in this edition.)

4. A GIRAFFE HAS ___ BONES IN ITS NECK – THE SAME AS A HUMAN.

(Number of white stars in this edition.)

5. THE LONGEST RETICULATED PYTHON EVER RECORDED WAS AROUND ____ METRES LONG.

(Number of grey stars in this edition.)

For the answer, see pages 148–150

SHAPE CHALLENGE

One morning as Rahim, Mae, Sasha and Angelo walked into their classroom, they noticed some shapes sketched on the board.

Mrs Page began to explain. “I’ve got a quick puzzle for you this morning as a brain warm up . . .”

Can you work out what connects the shapes to the numbers inside them, and what the missing numbers should be?

Hint:
WHAT DO YOU NOTICE ABOUT THE SHAPES?
IS THERE ANYTHING ABOUT THEM
THAT YOU CAN COUNT?

For the answer, see page 150

SCHOOL JOURNEYS

Angelo and Sasha both lived close enough to Whodunnit High to walk to school – Mae, though, lived a little further away.

"I've got three choices of which vehicle to use to get to school," she said to the others. "How about a challenge? Here are all of the letters of the three vehicles."

I S B I T C U E R

N Y A L B C

Can you make the names of three vehicles from the scattered letters and complete the names below? Use each letter only once, and don't leave any letters out! The first letters have been filled in already and crossed out in Mae's list.

B _ _ _ _ _ _

T _ _ _ _

B _ _

Hint:

WHAT VEHICLE NAMES CAN YOU THINK OF? CAN YOU SPELL ANY OF THEM USING THE LETTERS ON THE OPPOSITE PAGE?

For the answer, see page 150

TREETOP TASK

Mae had been reading a book all about the rainforest, and the animals that live there – and she was thrilled to discover a puzzle when she was halfway through!

Can you help Mae finish the wordsearch? All of the words are either hidden horizontally (across) or vertically (up and down).

Bonus question:
Which animal from the wordsearch opposite is a type of snake?

J	A	G	U	A	R	W	O	Y	M	T	F
K	W	K	Q	X	M	N	T	I	G	E	R
C	A	P	Y	B	A	R	A	M	S	M	P
E	P	A	I	Y	N	R	V	C	T	W	A
K	A	N	O	R	A	N	G	U	T	A	N
A	R	T	T	S	C	T	T	P	A	S	G
S	R	E	C	L	O	R	W	M	Y	I	O
T	O	A	N	O	N	G	L	M	M	E	L
A	T	T	T	T	D	S	G	E	J	A	I
P	S	E	K	H	A	T	O	U	C	A	N
I	E	R	P	U	P	C	B	T	M	U	Z
R	P	A	R	A	K	E	E	T	M	Q	A

ANACONDA
ANTEATER
CAPYBARA
JAGUAR
ORANGUTAN
PANGOLIN
PARAKEET
PARROT
SLOTH
TAPIR
TIGER
TOUCAN

For the answer, see page 151

ROOM RIDDLE

Mae was having a busy day! She had been dashing between rooms along one of Whodunnit High's many corridors as she went to different classes, clubs and to deliver things to people.

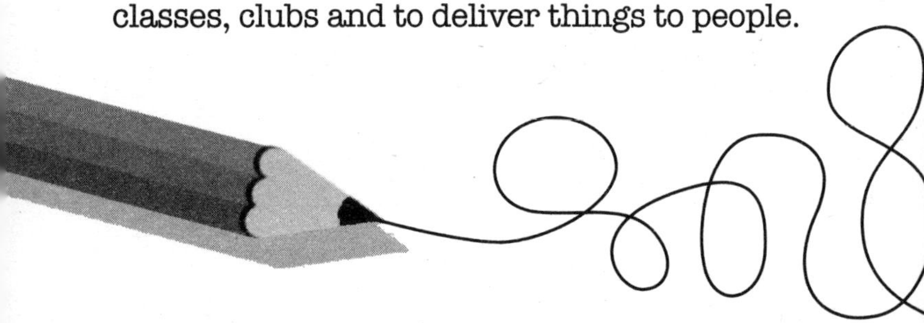

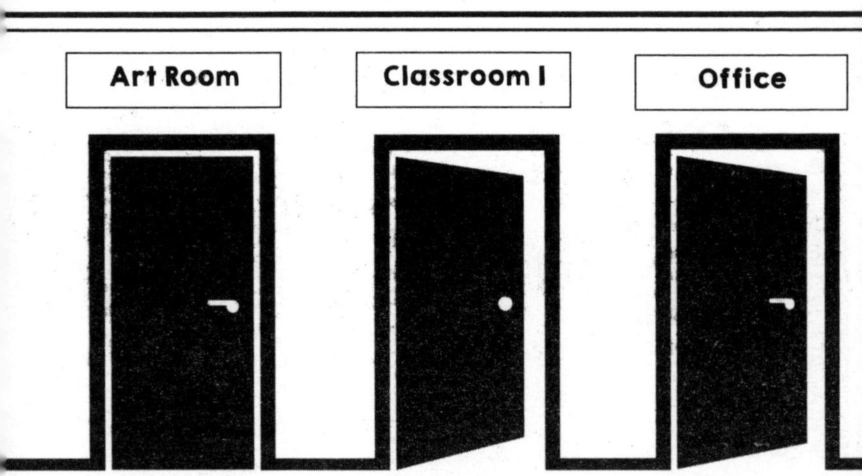

Can you use these notes on her route to work out the final room that Mae visited?

Mae started at the Computer Room.
She then went four rooms to the left.
She then went two rooms to the right.
She then went one room to the right.
She then went two rooms to the left.
She then went one room to the left.

Bonus question:
Which room did Mae NOT visit on her route?

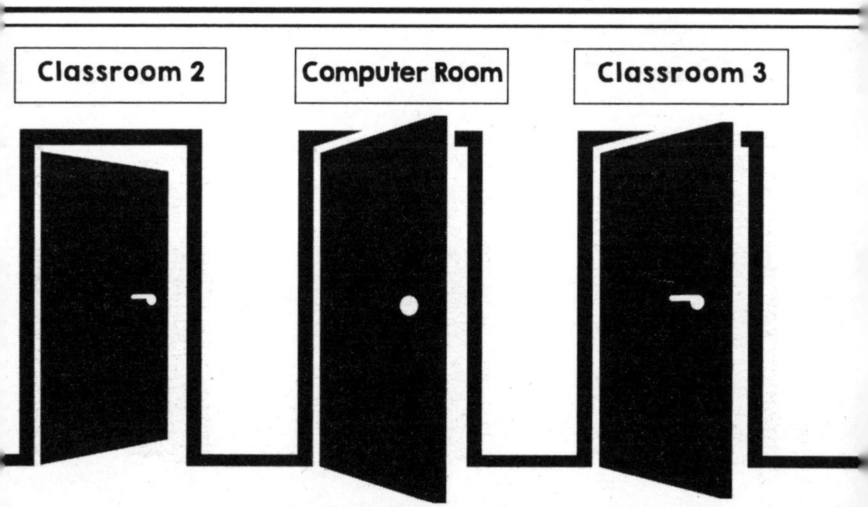

For the answer, see page 151

CROSSWORD COLLECTORS – 5

Ms Singh had given the four friends her fifth and final crossword! (See pages 18, 50, 78 and 88 for the other four.)

Can you complete it? Solve the numbered clues, then put your answers into the boxes in the grid that start with the matching number. The 'across' clues go horizontally, the 'down' clues go vertically.

Make a note of the letter in the shaded box! There are five crosswords in this book – find all the shaded letters, then put them together in the order they appear to reveal a hidden word.

Across

1. Leaf-eating larva of a butterfly (11)
6. Nut that grows into an oak tree (5)
7. Cherished (5)
9. Slime (3)
10. What the words 'cat' and 'mat' do (5)
12. Fish-eating river animal with brown fur (5)
14. Tool used for digging (5)
17. Break out of an egg (5)
19. Fail to tell the truth (3)
20. Honking waterbirds (5)
21. Sour yellow fruit (5)
23. Honest; reliable (11)

Down

1. Seat (5)
2. Also (3)
3. Extent or scope (5)
4. House made from blocks of solid snow (5)
5. Person on a horse or bicycle (5)
8. Animal doctor (3)
11. Wet dirt (3)
13. Popular hot drink (3)
14. Vision (5)
15. Large primate such as a gorilla or orangutan (3)
16. Choose a politician for office (5)
17. Common greeting word (5)
18. Sweet substance made by bees (5)
22. Came across (3)

For the answer, see page 152

SUNSHINE MYSTERY

It was a beautiful sunny day at Whodunnit High. Mae and Sasha were having an IT lesson with Mr Nelson, watching the sun stream in through the blinds – and secretly quite looking forward to being able to get outside at the end of the day.

"Are you doing anything after school today?" asked Mae. "I feel like planning something . . ."

Sasha was sitting opposite, with her computer screen facing away from Mae – she seemed to be very busy doing something, but Mae wasn't sure what . . .

Suddenly, she heard the classroom printer whirr into life.

"How about this for an idea?" Sasha said, passing her a piece of paper.

LET'S GET ICE CREAM

Can you work out what the message says?

Hint:

TRY HOLDING THE BOOK IN DIFFERENT POSITIONS.

For the answer, see page 152

READY, SET . . . LOGIC!

Mae, Angelo, Sasha and Rahim all competed in the school sports day. Can you work out which event each of them took part in, which team they represented and what place they came?

- **Mae was put in the red team.**
- **The child in the blue team won the relay race.**
- **Angelo competed in the ring toss.**
- **The child in the egg and spoon race did NOT come third.**
- **The child in the yellow team did not compete in the egg and spoon race.**
- **Rahim either came third or fourth in his event.**
- **The child in the green team came second in their event.**
- **Rahim was put in the yellow team.**

		Place				Team				Event			
		1st	2nd	3rd	4th	Blue	Green	Red	Yellow	Egg and spoon	Long jump	Relay race	Ring toss
Child	Angelo												
	Mae												
	Rahim												
	Sasha												
Event	Egg and spoon												
	Long jump												
	Relay race												
	Ring toss												
Team	Blue												
	Green												
	Red												
	Yellow												

FOR TIPS ON COMPLETING LOGIC PUZZLES, GO TO PAGE 156!

Child	Event	Team	Place
Angelo			
Mae			
Rahim			
Sasha			

For the answer, see page 153

THE WHODUNNIT PUZZLER

EDITION 6

Welcome to your favourite school newspaper.
All the news! All the updates! All the PUZZLES!

THE 'WRITE' IDEA

Do you think a rhyme is a brilliant time? Class 5A do! They tried their hand at writing their very own poems with local writer, Mira Patel. They all wrote about something that had made them laugh in the last week – Harry Bourne wrote his poem about a whoopie cushion that had been left on the school bus, and Laila Wen's rap about her little sister's potty training had everyone in stitches.

If you've written a poem, let us know! And don't forget to look out for the school poetry competition later this year.

TODAY'S PUZZLES ALSO HAVE A RHYMING THEME – GIVE THEM A GO AND SEE HOW YOU DO . . .

Can you solve these clues to reveal the sets of words? In every set, only one letter has been changed between each word – so all the words rhyme!

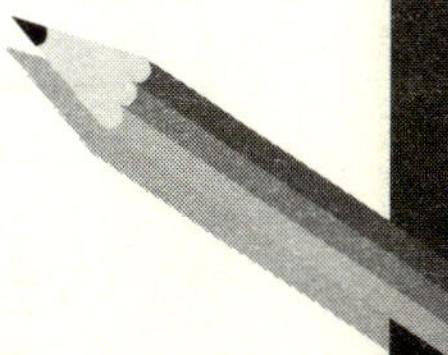

RHYME ONE

- Another name for a rabbit (5)
- Hilarious (5)
- A word for warm weather (5)

RHYME TWO

- A container, for example to hold baked beans (3)
- A place to put rubbish (3)
- Come first in a race (3)

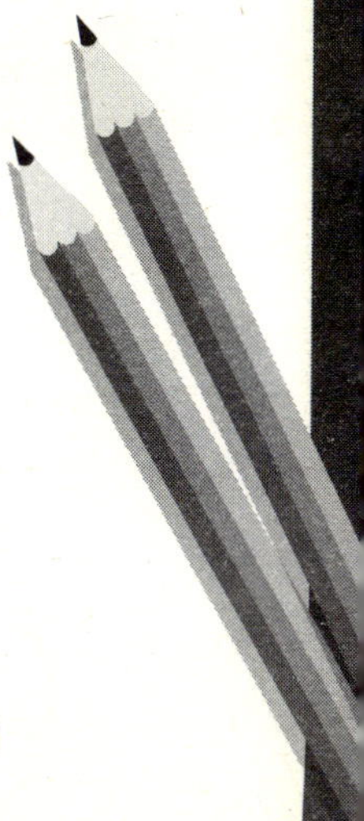

RHYME THREE

- The opposite of short (4)
- A structure made of bricks (4)
- Something you'd kick in a football game (4)

RHYME FOUR

- A sheep-like animal with horns (4)
- A vehicle used for sailing (4)
- Something you wear in cold weather (4)

For the answer, see page 153

A COMPUTER CONUNDRUM – PART 1

It was nearly the end of term at Whodunnit High – but there were a couple more puzzles still to come!

The four friends had been chatting while walking along the corridor by the school computer room, when they noticed something odd . . . the light in the computer room was off, but a single screen had been left on. Mr Nelson, the IT teacher, was strict about asking students to turn off their screens when they were done.

They walked over to the screen and saw that a document had been left open. But they couldn't immediately make out what it said.

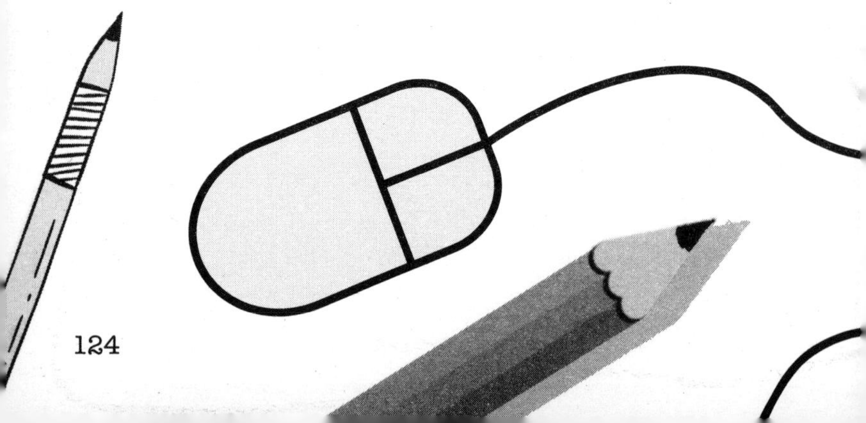

Can you find the message that has been hidden in the document?

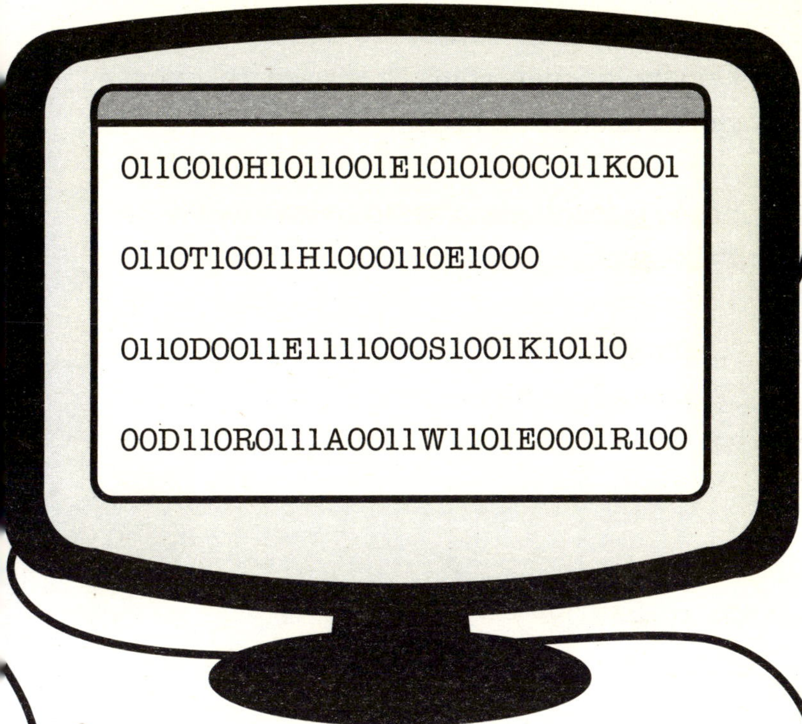

Hint:

EACH LINE HAS LOTS OF 1S AND 0S IN IT - BUT ARE THEY THE ONLY THING? WHAT ELSE CAN YOU SEE?

For the answer, see page 153

A COMPUTER CONUNDRUM – PART 2

The four quickly dashed to the desk drawer – it easily slid open when they tried. Inside was a sheet of folded up paper. When they unfurled it, they found a maze. And it wasn't just any maze . . . along the different twists and turns of the maze were letters.

"There must be a secret message hidden in it!" cried Rahim.

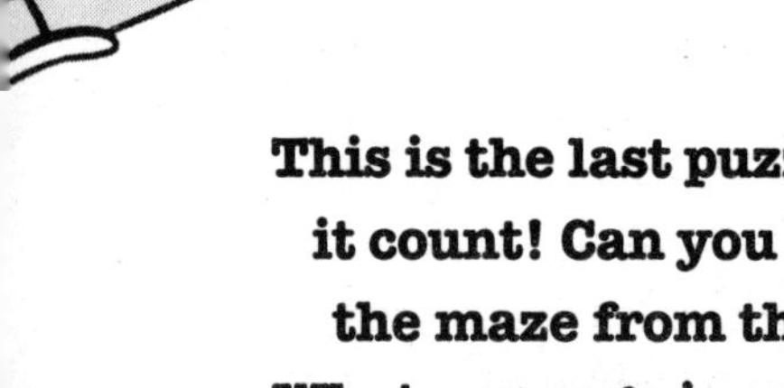

This is the last puzzle of term – let's make it count! Can you find the path through the maze from the start to the finish? What message is spelled out by the letters you collect along the way?

START

FINISH

For the answer, see page 154

CHALLENGE COMPLETED!

You've made it to the end – congratulations from Sasha, Rahim, Mae and Angelo on all your hard work and becoming a true Whodunnit High puzzler!

Hold on a second – another mysterious note has appeared . . . maybe it's not the end after all.

For all your hard work, you have been awarded a Whodunnit High certificate – but there's one final challenge . . . someone has hidden it! You just need to work out who has taken it and where they have hidden it.

Luckily for you, there are clues – this symbol appears next to the hider's name throughout this book:

Better go back and track them down!

Do you know who it is? Write the hider's name here, with no spaces.

Name: _ _ _ _ _ _ _

But where is it? Use the grid to find out. For each letter you've written above next to 'Name', find the corresponding letter or number from the white boxes in the grid. Write them down below to reveal the hiding place.

Hiding place: _ _ _ _ _ _ _

The correct name will reveal the hiding place!

A	B	C	D	E	F	G	H	I	J	K	L	M
1	D	R	L	O	Q	6	8	N	T	4	K	P

N	O	P	Q	R	S	T	U	V	W	X	Y	Z
5	1	E	7	A	G	F	3	U	H	2	P	V

For the answer, see page 155

ANSWERS

THE LUNCHBOX MYSTERY

A flapjack is missing.

THE LUNCHBOX MYSTERY – PART 2

The note is an acrostic – the first letter of each line spells out 'MIA BROWN'. Mae found Mia, who apologised – the two then shared the lunchbox.

THE MUSIC CLUB MYSTERY

A piano.

CROSSWORD COLLECTORS – 1

	1 U	2 M	B	3 R	E	4 L	L	5 A		
		O		E		I		L		
6 F	L	U	T	E		7 Q	U	I	C	8 K
R		S		K		U		E		A
9 E	V	E	N		10 D	I	N	N	E	R
E				11 A		D				A
12 D	E	13 M	A	N	D		14 Z	15 E	R	O
O		I		C		16 O		X		K
17 M	O	N	T	H		18 P	E	A	C	E
		U		O		E		C		
		19 S	T	R	E	N	G	T	H	

THE PRANK

The note says:

THE FOOTBALL KIT IS HIDDEN ON THE TOP SHELF OF THE EQUIPMENT CUPBOARD, BEHIND A BOX OF TENNIS BALLS.

It is written in mirror-writing – if you hold the message up to a mirror, or a reflective surface, you can read it normally.

THE SECRET COPYARTIST

A MYSTERY LIST

The first list contains words that are spelled the same if you read them forwards as they are when they are read backwards – like Hannah's name. The word from list two that could also fit into list one is REDDER.

ART ADVENTURES

Child	Subject	Material	Colour
Angelo	Fruit bowl	Felt tip	Pink
Mae	Sunflower	Pencil	Blue
Rahim	Self-portrait	Oil pastel	Green
Sasha	Tiger	Watercolour	Red

AROUND THE WORLD RIDDLING

It's a stamp! They can travel to another country on a parcel or letter, but always stay in the corner they have been stuck onto.

PAIR OF PENS

The matching pens are B and C.

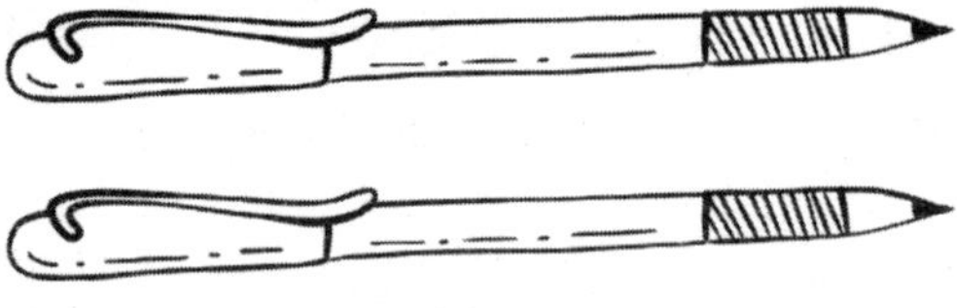

ANCIENT ADVENTURES

T	E	A	K	J	V	E	S	I	N	R	L
M	S	P	H	I	N	X	C	S	I	E	O
T	J	X	Z	P	S	I	A	F	L	C	B
P	H	A	R	A	O	H	R	O	E	H	E
M	D	P	B	P	H	H	A	M	Y	N	L
P	O	T	L	Y	P	X	B	Y	P	R	I
Y	H	I	E	R	O	G	L	Y	P	H	S
R	M	A	V	U	Y	C	Y	S	G	Y	K
A	U	D	E	S	E	R	T	I	V	E	H
M	M	L	C	R	O	C	O	D	I	L	E
I	M	Z	L	R	R	P	G	S	U	R	A
D	Y	E	P	J	A	C	K	A	L	P	E

MORSE CODE

A PAINTER.

THE WHODUNNIT PUZZLER – EDITION 1

Pets

1. DOG
2. CAT
3. HORSE
4. RABBIT
5. MOUSE

Wild Land Animals

1. GIRAFFE
2. BEAR
3. TIGER
4. LION
5. PANDA

Ocean Animals

1. SHARK
2. OCTOPUS
3. WHALE
4. DOLPHIN
5. TURTLE

JIGSAW CHALLENGE

The missing jigsaw pieces are D and H.

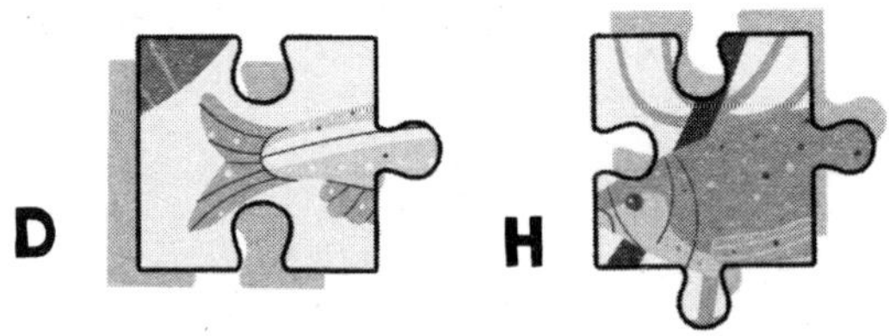

EMOJI CODE

The words are:

1. MARS
2. JUPITER
3. SATURN
4. CHICKEN
5. NEPTUNE

The odd one out is CHICKEN – this is a bird; all of the other words are names of planets in our Solar System.

IT ALL ADDS UP – PART 1

The four-digit code is 9238. The solutions to the sums are:

20 – 2 = 18
18 ÷ 3 = 6
6 + 3 = 9

4 x 4 = 16
16 + 4 = 20
20 ÷ 10 = 2

9 + 3 = 12
12 x 2 = 24
24 – 9 = 15
15 ÷ 5 = 3

14 ÷ 2 = 7
7 + 3 = 10
10 x 2 = 20
20 – 12 = 8

IT ALL ADDS UP – PART 2

The animal is a SHEEP. The first letter, 'S' is in SIT, but not in TIN – all the other letters are shared. If you follow the other clues in the same way, the word 'SHEEP' is revealed.

LIBRARY LOGIC

Child	Character	Setting	Genre
Angelo	Writer	Forest	Fantasy
Mae	Inventor	City	Non fiction
Rahim	Explorer	Mountain	Comedy
Sasha	Artist	Boat	Action

HOME TIME

An analogue clock.

CROSSWORD COLLECTORS – 2

1 C	H	2 O	C	3 O	L	4 A	T	5 E		
		N		C		T		N		
6 U	N	C	L	E		7 L	I	T	R	8 E
N		E		A		A		I		N
I				9 N	10 O	S	T	R	I	L
C		11 A			A			E		A
12 O	R	C	H	13 A	R	14 D				R
R		C		H		A		15 S		G
16 N	I	E	C	E		17 I	M	A	G	E
		P		A		L		V		
		18 T	E	D	D	Y	B	E	A	R

OPPOSITES

The opposite pairs for the first list are:

NOISY and QUIET

TALL and SHORT

FAST and SLOW

WET and DRY

The word without an opposite is BEST – its opposite would be WORST.

The opposite pairs for the second list are:

DARK and LIGHT

HIGH and LOW

AWAKE and ASLEEP

UP and DOWN

The word without an opposite is FRIENDS – its opposite would be ENEMIES.

When they are put together, the two words without opposites spell 'BEST FRIENDS' – describing the group!

ODD JUMPER OUT

The odd jumper out is D – the school badge is bigger than the others.

HIDDEN HABITAT

The words with missing double letters are:

1. LADDER (something you might use to climb up a wall)
2. SLEEP (you usually do this at night)
3. SCISSORS (a cutting tool)
4. KNEE (part of the human body, in the middle of the leg)
5. MIRROR (you can use this to look at yourself)
6. KITTEN (a baby cat)

The missing repeated letters are D, E, S, E, R and T – spelling 'DESERT'.

EXPLORATION EXCITEMENT

G	A	D	T	E	L	E	S	C	O	P	E
C	O	U	R	A	G	E	X	D	S	Z	T
C	T	A	E	S	M	A	P	I	Z	F	T
O	V	O	A	U	Q	U	E	S	T	T	S
M	D	S	S	R	U	T	P	C	C	U	S
P	T	O	U	V	R	T	Y	O	P	I	A
A	A	G	R	I	C	U	J	V	Y	T	K
S	T	S	E	V	Q	G	R	E	F	S	Y
S	P	R	T	A	J	O	U	R	N	E	Y
G	F	C	O	L	E	U	Y	Y	E	E	A
W	M	M	O	U	N	T	A	I	N	L	R
V	O	Y	A	G	E	S	U	M	M	I	T

Bonus question: The tool is a compass.

A MYSTERY BOOK – PART 1

The completed sequences are:

1. 12, 10, 8, 6, 4, 2 – taking away two each time.
2. 6, 9, 12, 15, 18, 21 – adding three each time.
3. 7, 12, 17, 22, 27, 32 – adding five each time.
4. 2, 4, 8, 16, 32, 64 – multiplying by two each time.

In the order they appear, the circled numbers are: 2, 9, 7, 8. So, the padlock code is 2978.

A MYSTERY BOOK - PART 2

The name hidden in the grid is MAE. This book would be easy for Angelo to return to its owner!

THE WHODUNNIT PUZZLER – EDITION 2

Citrus fruit

1. LEMON
2. ORANGE
3. LIME
4. GRAPEFRUIT

Tropical fruit

1. MANGO
2. WATERMELON
3. BANANA
4. PAPAYA

Berries

1. STRAWBERRY
2. RASPBERRY
3. CRANBERRY
4. BLUEBERRY

THE HIDDEN NOTE

The voucher is hidden in the book called *Space Travels.*

QUIZ WIZARDS

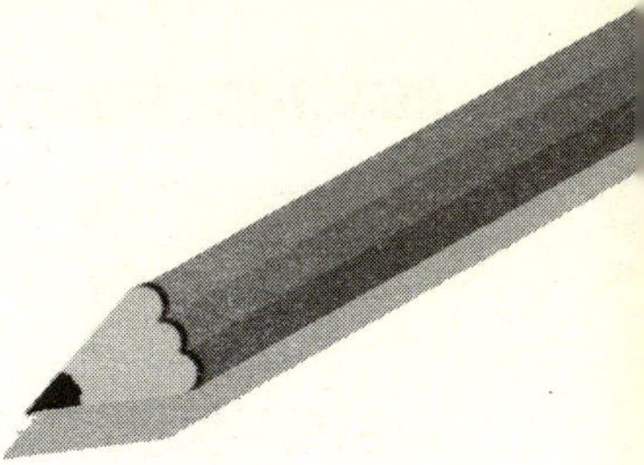

The answers are:

1. SNAKE
2. SIX
3. PURPLE
4. FOAL
5. EGYPT

The grey boxes spell out the word SILLY!

LUNCH LOGIC

Child	Sandwich	Fruit	Treat
Angelo	Cheese	Kiwi	Cupcake
Mae	Jam	Apple	Flapjack
Rahim	Cucumber	Orange	Popcorn
Sasha	Ham	Peach	Chocolate

DOUBLE TROUBLE

1. MOUSE
2. BAT
3. BARK
4. PUPIL

DEADLY DINOSAURS

D	T	R	I	C	E	R	A	T	O	P	S
D	R	E	J	U	R	A	S	S	I	C	T
I	Z	P	R	E	D	A	T	O	R	S	E
P	T	E	R	O	D	A	C	T	Y	L	G
L	R	S	L	Q	C	N	D	F	T	R	O
O	I	G	U	A	N	O	D	O	N	A	S
D	A	N	P	U	L	N	S	S	L	P	A
O	S	C	L	A	W	S	V	S	Q	T	U
C	S	T	A	T	O	V	N	I	E	O	R
U	I	U	R	I	C	Z	R	L	W	R	U
S	C	L	E	P	P	U	N	R	F	T	S
O	X	E	X	T	I	N	C	T	Y	Z	Q

Bonus question: The three-horned dinosaur is the Triceratops.

THE WHODUNNIT PUZZLER – EDITION 3

Summer clothes

1. SHORTS
2. SUNHAT
3. SANDALS
4. VEST
5. SWIMSUIT
6. SUNGLASSES

Countries

1. NIGERIA
2. SWEDEN
3. CANADA
4. AUSTRALIA
5. PAKISTAN
6. POLAND

Weather

1. RAIN
2. SNOW
3. SUNSHINE
4. WIND
5. CLOUDY
6. BLIZZARD

CROSSWORD COLLECTORS – 3

1 N	U	2 I	S	A	3 N	C	4 E	■	5 H	■
O	■	N	■	■	E	■	N	■	A	■
6 R	E	E	F	■	7 A	U	T	U	M	8 N
T	■	P	■	■	R	■	E	■	■	I
9 H	U	T	10 C	H	■	11 W	R	O	N	G
P	■	■	L	■	■	■	E	■	■	H
12 O	N	I	O	N	■	13 A	D	14 M	I	T
L	■	■	T	■	15 H	■	■	E	■	M
16 E	17 I	G	H	T	Y	■	18 E	L	S	A
■	C	■	E	■	M	■	■	O	■	R
■	E	■	19 S	E	N	T	E	N	C	E

TANGLED UP

Ball 1 – RAHIM
Ball 2 – ANGELO
Ball 3 – SASHA
Ball 4 – MAE

MINIBEAST MYSTERY

All five names are spelled backwards in the list. Decoded, the five insects are:

1. WASP
2. GRASSHOPPER
3. BEE
4. BUTTERFLY
5. MOSQUITO

THE FINGERPRINTS

The missing fingerprint belongs to Mae.

SHOE CONFUSION

The correct pairs are:

A and H

E and F

B and D

C and G.

CROSSWORD COLLECTORS – 4

1 C	I	N	D	2 E	R	3 E	L	4 L	A	■
A	■	■	■	X	■	A	■	E	■	■
5 M	U	6 S	I	C	■	7 S	P	I	K	8 E
E	■	P	■	E	■	T	■	C	■	N
9 L	E	A	D	E	R	■	10 B	E	N	D
■	■	G	■	D	■	11 P	■	S	■	■
12 E	C	H	O	■	13 B	O	T	T	O	14 M
A	■	E	■	15 N	■	T	■	E	■	O
16 T	I	T	L	E	■	17 A	P	R	O	N
■	■	T	■	S	■	T	■	■	■	E
■	18 D	I	C	T	I	O	N	A	R	Y

SPACE SOLVERS – PART 1

A	S	T	R	O	N	A	U	T	H	A	A
Y	M	S	S	T	A	R	F	R	T	R	N
T	O	U	O	A	S	T	E	R	O	I	D
S	O	P	U	B	M	P	T	R	H	F	F
P	N	E	P	L	E	Q	M	A	X	Z	I
T	O	R	S	A	T	E	L	L	I	T	E
D	G	N	X	C	E	O	E	I	B	R	O
I	A	O	U	K	O	N	O	R	B	I	T
U	L	V	T	H	R	S	M	I	U	L	V
I	A	A	P	O	I	Z	C	O	M	E	T
T	X	P	T	L	T	F	U	E	L	A	T
E	Y	E	V	E	E	P	L	A	N	E	T

SPACE SOLVERS – PART TWO

1. AN ASTRONAUT
2. PLANET
3. AN ASTEROID
4. A TELESCOPE
5. THE MOON

The word spelled by the circled letters is ALIEN!

AWAY ON HOLIDAY

Child	Country	Type of holiday	Souvenir
Angelo	Spain	Hiking	Bracelet
Mae	Scotland	Hotel resort	Pencil
Rahim	Wales	Beach	Notebook
Sasha	France	Camping	Key ring

THE LOST PENCIL CASE – PART 1

The note says:
I BELONG TO CARLA PEREZ

In the code, each letter in the alphabet has an equivalent number, matching its position in the alphabet, as shown in Rahim's chart. A=1, B=2, and so on.

THE LOST PENCIL CASE – PART 2

The message is a joke! It says:

WHAT GAME DO CROCODILES LIKE PLAYING?
SNAP!

SPORTS CHALLENGE

There are nine footballs, 16 tennis balls and 11 basketballs.

Bonus question: The only type of ball with an even number in the cupboard is the tennis ball.

SECRET NOTE

Present idea one is a T SHIRT. Present idea two is a DIARY.

If you just read the letters in squares in order, they spell 'T SHIRT'. If you just read the circled letters in order, they spell 'DIARY'.

THE WHODUNNIT PUZZLER – EDITION 5

1. An octopus has three hearts.

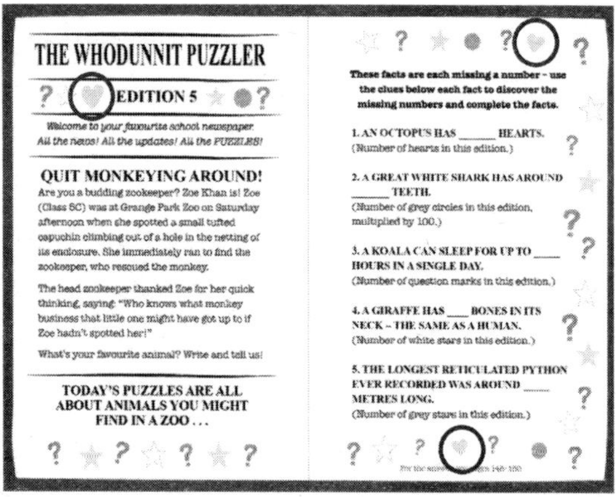

THE WHODUNNIT PUZZLER

EDITION 5

Welcome to your favourite school newspaper. All the news! All the updates! All the PUZZLES!

QUIT MONKEYING AROUND!

Are you a budding zookeeper? Zoe Khan is! Zoe (Class 5C) was at Grange Park Zoo on Saturday afternoon when she spotted a small tufted capuchin climbing out of a hole in the netting of its enclosure. She immediately ran to find the zookeeper, who rescued the monkey.

The head zookeeper thanked Zoe for her quick thinking, saying: "Who knows what monkey business that little one might have got up to if Zoe hadn't spotted her!"

What's your favourite animal? Write and tell us!

TODAY'S PUZZLES ARE ALL ABOUT ANIMALS YOU MIGHT FIND IN A ZOO . . .

These facts are each missing a number – use the clues below each fact to discover the missing numbers and complete the facts.

1. AN OCTOPUS HAS _____ HEARTS. (Number of hearts in this edition.)

2. A GREAT WHITE SHARK HAS AROUND _____ TEETH. (Number of grey circles in this edition, multiplied by 100.)

3. A KOALA CAN SLEEP FOR UP TO _____ HOURS IN A SINGLE DAY. (Number of question marks in this edition.)

4. A GIRAFFE HAS ____ BONES IN ITS NECK – THE SAME AS A HUMAN. (Number of white stars in this edition.)

5. THE LONGEST RETICULATED PYTHON EVER RECORDED WAS AROUND _____ METRES LONG. (Number of grey stars in this edition.)

For the answers, see pages 148–150.

2. A great white shark has around 300 teeth.

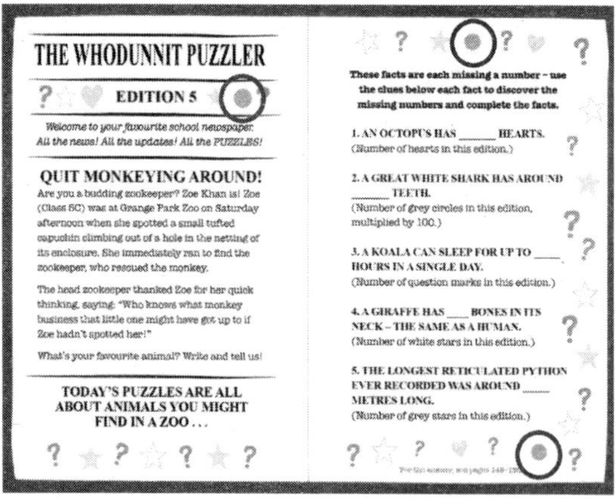

THE WHODUNNIT PUZZLER

EDITION 5

Welcome to your favourite school newspaper. All the news! All the updates! All the PUZZLES!

QUIT MONKEYING AROUND!

Are you a budding zookeeper? Zoe Khan is! Zoe (Class 5C) was at Grange Park Zoo on Saturday afternoon when she spotted a small tufted capuchin climbing out of a hole in the netting of its enclosure. She immediately ran to find the zookeeper, who rescued the monkey.

The head zookeeper thanked Zoe for her quick thinking, saying: "Who knows what monkey business that little one might have got up to if Zoe hadn't spotted her!"

What's your favourite animal? Write and tell us!

TODAY'S PUZZLES ARE ALL ABOUT ANIMALS YOU MIGHT FIND IN A ZOO . . .

These facts are each missing a number – use the clues below each fact to discover the missing numbers and complete the facts.

1. AN OCTOPUS HAS _____ HEARTS. (Number of hearts in this edition.)

2. A GREAT WHITE SHARK HAS AROUND _____ TEETH. (Number of grey circles in this edition, multiplied by 100.)

3. A KOALA CAN SLEEP FOR UP TO _____ HOURS IN A SINGLE DAY. (Number of question marks in this edition.)

4. A GIRAFFE HAS ____ BONES IN ITS NECK – THE SAME AS A HUMAN. (Number of white stars in this edition.)

5. THE LONGEST RETICULATED PYTHON EVER RECORDED WAS AROUND _____ METRES LONG. (Number of grey stars in this edition.)

For the answers, see pages 148–150.

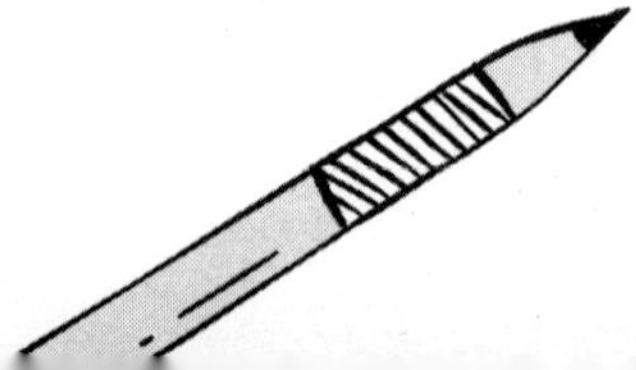

3. A koala can sleep for up to 18 hours in a single day.

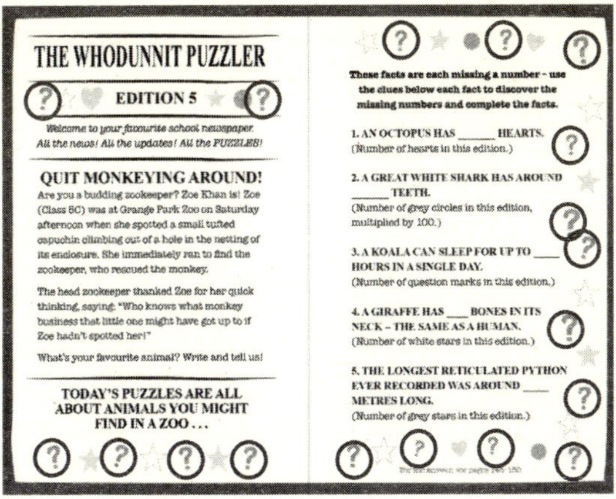

THE WHODUNNIT PUZZLER

EDITION 5

Welcome to your favourite school newspaper. All the news! All the updates! All the PUZZLES!

QUIT MONKEYING AROUND!

Are you a budding zookeeper? Zoe Khan is! Zoe (Class 5C) was at Grange Park Zoo on Saturday afternoon when she spotted a small tufted capuchin climbing out of a hole in the netting of its enclosure. She immediately ran to find the zookeeper, who rescued the monkey.

The head zookeeper thanked Zoe for her quick thinking, saying: "Who knows what monkey business that little one might have got up to if Zoe hadn't spotted her!"

What's your favourite animal? Write and tell us!

TODAY'S PUZZLES ARE ALL ABOUT ANIMALS YOU MIGHT FIND IN A ZOO . . .

These facts are each missing a number – use the clues below each fact to discover the missing numbers and complete the facts.

1. AN OCTOPUS HAS ______ HEARTS.
(Number of hearts in this edition.)

2. A GREAT WHITE SHARK HAS AROUND ______ TEETH.
(Number of grey circles in this edition, multiplied by 100.)

3. A KOALA CAN SLEEP FOR UP TO ____ HOURS IN A SINGLE DAY.
(Number of question marks in this edition.)

4. A GIRAFFE HAS ____ BONES IN ITS NECK – THE SAME AS A HUMAN.
(Number of white stars in this edition.)

5. THE LONGEST RETICULATED PYTHON EVER RECORDED WAS AROUND ____ METRES LONG.
(Number of grey stars in this edition.)

4. A giraffe has seven bones in its neck – the same as a human.

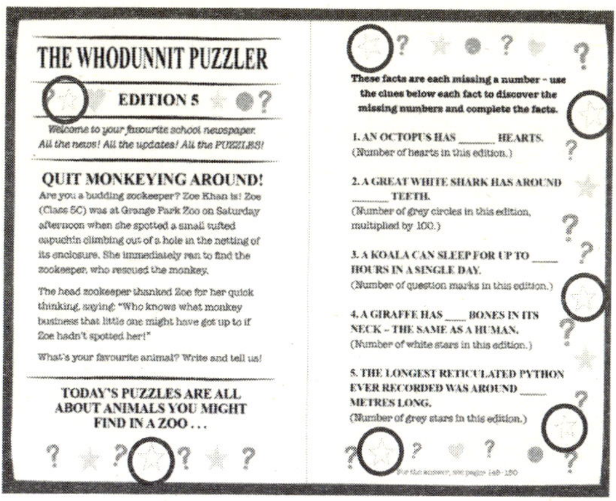

THE WHODUNNIT PUZZLER

EDITION 5

Welcome to your favourite school newspaper. All the news! All the updates! All the PUZZLES!

QUIT MONKEYING AROUND!

Are you a budding zookeeper? Zoe Khan is! Zoe (Class 5C) was at Grange Park Zoo on Saturday afternoon when she spotted a small tufted capuchin climbing out of a hole in the netting of its enclosure. She immediately ran to find the zookeeper, who rescued the monkey.

The head zookeeper thanked Zoe for her quick thinking, saying: "Who knows what monkey business that little one might have got up to if Zoe hadn't spotted her!"

What's your favourite animal? Write and tell us!

TODAY'S PUZZLES ARE ALL ABOUT ANIMALS YOU MIGHT FIND IN A ZOO . . .

These facts are each missing a number – use the clues below each fact to discover the missing numbers and complete the facts.

1. AN OCTOPUS HAS ______ HEARTS.
(Number of hearts in this edition.)

2. A GREAT WHITE SHARK HAS AROUND ______ TEETH.
(Number of grey circles in this edition, multiplied by 100.)

3. A KOALA CAN SLEEP FOR UP TO ____ HOURS IN A SINGLE DAY.
(Number of question marks in this edition.)

4. A GIRAFFE HAS ____ BONES IN ITS NECK – THE SAME AS A HUMAN.
(Number of white stars in this edition.)

5. THE LONGEST RETICULATED PYTHON EVER RECORDED WAS AROUND ____ METRES LONG.
(Number of grey stars in this edition.)

5. The reticulated python can grow over six metres long.

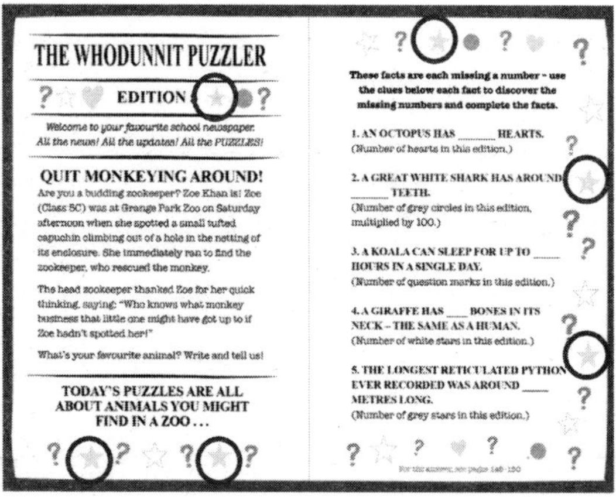

THE WHODUNNIT PUZZLER

EDITION

Welcome to your favourite school newspaper. All the news! All the updates! All the PUZZLES!

QUIT MONKEYING AROUND!

Are you a budding zookeeper? Zoe Khan is! Zoe (Class 5C) was at Grange Park Zoo on Saturday afternoon when she spotted a small tufted capuchin climbing out of a hole in the netting of its enclosure. She immediately ran to find the zookeeper, who rescued the monkey.

The head zookeeper thanked Zoe for her quick thinking, saying: "Who knows what monkey business that little one might have got up to if Zoe hadn't spotted her!"

What's your favourite animal? Write and tell us!

TODAY'S PUZZLES ARE ALL ABOUT ANIMALS YOU MIGHT FIND IN A ZOO . . .

These facts are each missing a number – use the clues below each fact to discover the missing numbers and complete the facts.

1. AN OCTOPUS HAS ______ HEARTS.
(Number of hearts in this edition.)

2. A GREAT WHITE SHARK HAS AROUND ______ TEETH.
(Number of grey circles in this edition, multiplied by 100.)

3. A KOALA CAN SLEEP FOR UP TO ______ HOURS IN A SINGLE DAY.
(Number of question marks in this edition.)

4. A GIRAFFE HAS ____ BONES IN ITS NECK – THE SAME AS A HUMAN.
(Number of white stars in this edition.)

5. THE LONGEST RETICULATED PYTHON EVER RECORDED WAS AROUND ______ METRES LONG.
(Number of grey stars in this edition.)

SHAPE CHALLENGE

The numbers inside the shapes match the number of sides that each shape has – the triangle has three sides, the rectangle has four sides, and so on.

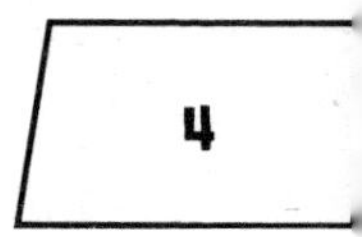

The missing numbers are 4 and 5.

SCHOOL JOURNEYS

The vehicles are a BICYCLE, TRAIN and BUS.

TREETOP TASK

J	A	G	U	A	R	W	O	Y	M	T	F
K	W	K	Q	X	M	N	T	I	G	E	R
C	A	P	Y	B	A	R	A	M	S	M	P
E	P	A	I	Y	N	R	V	C	T	W	A
K	A	N	O	R	A	N	G	U	T	A	N
A	R	T	T	S	C	T	T	P	A	S	G
S	R	E	C	L	O	R	W	M	Y	I	O
T	O	A	N	O	N	G	L	M	M	E	L
A	T	T	T	T	D	S	G	E	J	A	I
P	S	E	K	H	A	T	O	U	C	A	N
I	E	R	P	U	P	C	B	T	M	U	Z
R	P	A	R	A	K	E	E	T	M	Q	A

Bonus question: An anaconda is a type of snake.

ROOM RIDDLE

The final room that Mae visited was the Art Room. She did not visit Classroom 3. Her route was:

1. Computer Room
2. Art Room
3. Office
4. Classroom 2
5. Classroom 1
6. Art Room

CROSSWORD COLLECTORS – 5

1 C	A	2 T	E	3 R	P	4 I	L	L	A	5 R
H		O		A		G				I
6 A	C	O	R	N		7 L	O	8 V	E	D
I				9 G	O	O		E		E
10 R	H	Y	11 M	E		12 O	13 T	T	E	R
			U				E			
14 S	P	15 A	D	16 E		17 H	A	T	C (shaded)	18 H
I		P		19 L	I	E				O
20 G	E	E	S	E		21 L	E	22 M	O	N
H				C		L		E		E
23 T	R	U	S	T	W	O	R	T	H	Y

The hidden word spelled out by all the shaded squares in the five crosswords is MAGIC.

SUNSHINE MYSTERY

The note says LET'S GET ICE CREAM. To read it, hold the book flat and facing up, and look at the message from the bottom of the page.

READY, SET . . . LOGIC!

Child	Event	Team	Place
Angelo	Ring toss	Green	2nd
Mae	Egg & spoon	Red	4th
Rahim	Long jump	Yellow	3rd
Sasha	Relay race	Blue	1st

THE WHODUNNIT PUZZLER – EDITION 6

1.
BUNNY
FUNNY
SUNNY

2.
TIN
BIN
WIN

3.
TALL
WALL
BALL

4.
GOAT
BOAT
COAT

A COMPUTER CONUNDRUM – PART 1

The hidden message is: CHECK THE DESK DRAWER. If you ignore all of the numbers and read just the letters in each line, this message is revealed.

A COMPUTER CONUNDRUM – PART 2

The correct route through the maze is:

In order, the route passes through the letters W, E, L, L, D, O, N and E – spelling . . .

WELL DONE!

CHALLENGE COMPLETED

Mrs Page hid the certificate – the school symbol  is next to her name throughout the book.

The certificate is hidden on page 160. Using the grid, M=P, R=A, S=G, P=E, A=1, G=6 and E=0, spelling PAGE 160.

Name: M R S P A G E

Hiding place: P A G E 1 6 0

Go to the end of the book to collect your certificate!

LOGIC PUZZLES

To solve each one, you will be given a set of clues, a grid and boxes to fill in your answers.

Start by filling in the boxes with information from the clues. For example, in the puzzle on page 26, the first clue tells you that **Mae created her drawing in pencil**. So fill in the box like this:

Child	Subject	Material	Colour
Angelo			
Mae		PENCIL	
Rahim			
Sasha			

Then, tick the square in the grid where Mae's row meets the pencil column (shown below).

Mae used pencil, so you know nobody else did. Therefore, you can cross out the materials Mae didn't use (shown right). You can also add crosses to show the people who did NOT use pencil.

		Colour				Material			
		Blue	Green	Pink	Red	Felt tip	Oil pastel	Pencil	Watercolour
Child	Angelo							X	
	Mae					X	X	✓	X
	Rahim							X	
	Sasha							X	

The final clue tells you **Sasha painted her picture in watercolour**, so you can fill in the box and grid like you did for the first clue.

	Colour				Material			
Child	Blue	Green	Pink	Red	Felt tip	Oil pastel	Pencil	Watercolour
Angelo							X	X
Mae					X	X	✓	X
Rahim							X	X
Sasha					X	X	X	✓

The clues don't tell you what material Rahim or Angelo used, so you need to use logic. The four blank spaces left under 'Material' show that they used either felt tip or oil pastel.

Clue three on page 26 tells us that **Angelo's picture was pink**. Clue four tells us that the **green drawing was oil pastel**. Because Angelo's drawing was pink, it could not have been oil pastel – so, logically, it must be felt tip!

And Rahim used oil pastel because that is the only option left.

	Colour				Material			
Child	Blue	Green	Pink	Red	Felt tip	Oil pastel	Pencil	Watercolour
Angelo					✓	X	X	X
Mae					X	X	✓	X
Rahim					X	✓	X	X
Sasha					X	X	X	✓

Keep going through the clues to find out more – remember to keep filling in the answer boxes and the grid!

ALSO AVAILABLE

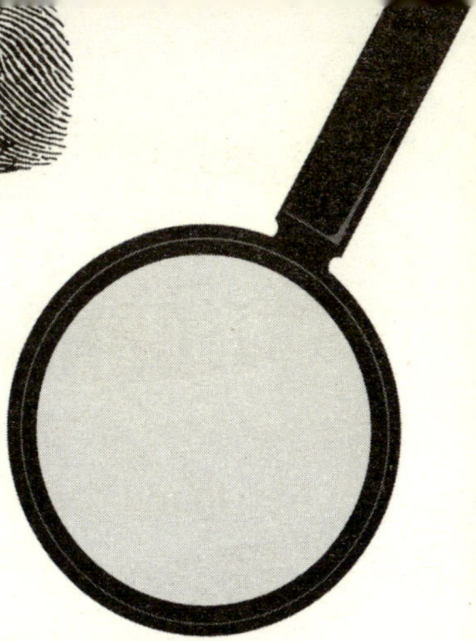

AMAZING
PUZZLES
&
QUIZZES
FOR EVERY
9
YEAR OLD

AMAZING
PUZZLES
&
QUIZZES
FOR EVERY
10
YEAR OLD

AMAZING
PUZZLES
&
QUIZZES
EASTER

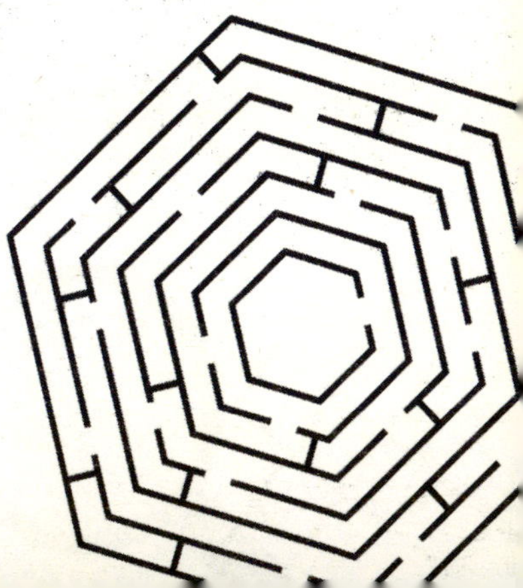

CONGRATULATIONS!

You found the certificate! It was Mrs Page who hid it . . . but she couldn't keep it from you!